LOVESTYLES:
HOW TO CELEBRATE YOUR DIFFERENCES

Tina B. Tessina, M.A.
Author of *How to Be a Couple and Still Be Free*

NEWCASTLE PUBLISHING CO., INC.
NORTH HOLLYWOOD, CALIFORNIA
1987

Edited by Douglas Menville
Cover/book design by Riley K. Smith

The concept of the "Script Onion," which appears in Part One, Chapter 3, is used with the permission of its creator, psychotherapist Denton L. Roberts.

Excerpts from the article, "Polygamy: Another Lovestyle," by Deborah Anapol, are used with the permission of the author.

Excerpts from the book, *Living in the Light*, by Shakti Gawain with Laurel King, are used with the permission of the authors.

FIRST EDITION

A NEWCASTLE BOOK
First printing April 1987
9 8 7 6 5 4 3 2 1
Printed in the United States of America

To the Inner Circle:
Maggie, Eddie, Riley,
Ron, Sylvia, Scott
and Richard,

who loved me through this.

Acknowledgments

My thanks to:

Newcastle Publishing and Al Saunders (whom Riley and I fondly call "the unconscious agent of the Aquarian Conspiracy"). Al is truly an honest and caring businessman, and I am proud to be associated with him. Also to his wife Daryl, who was among the first to read the manuscript.

Doug Menville, my extremely able, patient and encouraging editor, for service beyond the call of duty.

Riley K. Smith, for being there; for his creative and wonderful cover art and for proposing the final version of the title.

Ms. J. Kelley Younger, for her reading of the original MS (or is that mess?) and her excellent suggestions for improvement.

All my friends who read for me, especially Floyd Goff and Don Tobey, for their detailed editorial comments and suggestions.

My secretaries, Ann Henson and Kathi deMille, for cheerful and efficient service which allowed me time to write.

Peter McWilliams, for his encouragement and help with my computer purchase.

Last but not least, my dear friends, teachers, clients and students, who supported, encouraged, tested theories and demonstrated the ideas in these pages.

Contents

Preface ix

PART ONE: EXPLANATIONS 1
Introduction 3
Author's Note 6
1 Lovestyles 7
2 Love 9
3 Style 14
4 Communication 28
5 Synthesis 34

PART TWO: EXERCISES 47
Introduction 49
1 Defining and Discovering Your Own Lovestyle   52
    Section I: Origins of Lovestyles 53
                   Exercises for Individuals 54
                   Exercises for New Relationships . . 58
                   Exercises for Longterm
                       Relationships 65
    Section II: Your Individual, Unique Lovestyle   68
                   Exercises for Individuals 68
                   Exercises for New Relationships . . 76
                   Exercises for Longterm
                       Relationships 79
    Section III: Changes—Redesigning Your
                       Lovestyle
                   Exercises for Individuals 85

Exercises for New Relationships . . 96

Exercises for Longterm
    Relationships 100

2 Creating Communication: Sharing Lovestyles
    Effectively 106

    Section I: Sharing, Hearing, Keeping
                 the Balance 108

                 Exercises for Individuals 113

                 Exercises for New Relationships . . 123

                 Exercises for Longterm
                 Relationships 134

3 Synthesizing Lovestyles 144

    Section I: The Nitty Gritty: What You
                 Want/Need in Your Relation-
                 ship; Your Essential Individu-
                 ality of Style 145

                 Exercises for Individuals 147

                 Exercises for New Relationships . . 151

                 Exercises for Longterm
                 Relationships 156

    Section II: Brainstorming/Experimenting/
                 Celebrating 161

                 Exercises for Individuals 163

                 Exercises for New Relationships . . 170

                 Exercises for Longterm
                 Relationships 173

    Section III: Review and Clarify 177

                 Exercises for Individuals 177

                 Exercises for New Relationships . . 180

                 Exercises for Longterm
                 Relationships 182

    Section IV: The Toybox 184

    Section V: The Yardstick: An Evaluation
                 Process 186

PART THREE: EXPERIENCES 191
Introduction 193
1   Lifestyles 203
2   The Variety of Lifestyles and Some Problems
      with Them 205
3   The Etiquette of Alternative Relationships 209
4   Being Yourself in Society 223
5   Sample Lovestyles/Lifestyles 227

Reading Resources 276

PREFACE

IT WAS ONE of those magical encounters with a personal truth—you know how it feels. I was fifteen, in ninth-grade English. The teacher, Mr. Rizzutto, read us a poem, and it had such a profound effect on me that twenty-seven years later, I'm still using it as a guide. The poem, "Outwitted," by Edwin Markham, is simple:

> He drew a circle that shut me out;
> Heretic; rebel; a thing to flout.
> But Love and I had the wit to win:
> We drew a circle that took him in.

Learning to apply it in my life has not been simple, but it has been amazingly educational and rewarding. This book is about drawing the circle with love.

So much of my current health and happiness in life is possible because of writers of books: Louisa May Alcott, Ken Keyes, Shakti Gawain, Jane Roberts and Seth, Carl Rogers, Richard Bach, Thaddeus Golas and many, many other authors have helped shape my life and my thought.*

Now that I'd like to pass my own thoughts on, I think of my resistance to the ideas in all those books, and how some writers (even though they had wonderful ideas) seemed to reinforce my resistance and some seemed to slide right past. Even excellent information can be expressed in a critical, negative way—even (on occasion) by loving, positive people.

*For titles by these authors and others, see Reading Resources List.

My road has been forty-two years long now, and I have far to go. There was a time when life seemed very hard, so hard I tried not to think about it. It's easier now. Several times I helped to destroy some very viable relationships. I'm no longer doing much of that.

However, I still get unreasonable and angry. I still stand and "helplessly" watch myself do what I *know* will create a mess which later I'll have to clean up—but I do this much less often now. I still feel very human, and glad of it.

This book is not intended to help you become perfect— you and I already are. The object is to help your journey proceed on its way, and to make the hard places a little easier.

Changing myself, my life and my loves has been very exciting, and I'm very proud. My concern is that in hearing my pride and excitement, you may become discouraged because you see me as having "made it" and yourself as far behind.

We're all on the same path, and each of us has our own contributions and areas of expertise. This is mine. There are many things I have yet to learn, and even some of the things I already know could use more practice. Expressing love is an art. In art, you have never "made it"; you can always polish your craft, learn more, express yourself more clearly.

The most powerful technique I've learned is to be gentle with myself, and to appreciate every baby step I take. It's from this appreciation (I also call it celebration) of myself that I draw the energy and enthusiasm I need. From it comes my motivation to grow and to achieve more. From it also comes the trust that allows me more and more to live life as I find it, without needing to make it fit my plan.

My intention with the information in this book is to help you to be gentle with yourself and others and to help you celebrate. If you'll meet this book halfway and approach it with gentleness and forgiveness for your mistakes, we can create something wonderful together.

Tina Tessina
Long Beach, Calif.

PART ONE

EXPLANATIONS

INTRODUCTION

THROUGHOUT THE PROCESS of becoming more conscious and aware of myself, which began for me in about 1970, the truth has been that the important changes did not happen in great blinding flashes or dramatic moments in important workshops. Rather, they came in small, significant insights gained as I sat alone and pondered the ideas of my teachers in relationship to the facts of my life. Such a moment happened last year, as I was attemptig to sort out a difficulty between my husband Richard and myself.

We were having trouble entertaining. It was awkward, irritating and difficult. It never went smoothly. I had recently been in two long-lasting roommate situations, two years with Annie and two years with Ron, just before getting married. In both situations, entertaining had been fun and easy, right from the start. Why was it so difficult now? Was sex the problem? We weren't having trouble there, but it was the only major difference from roommate situations. Ron and Annie and I had entertained with such style. Aha! *Style!* That was it! I didn't know what Richard's and my style was! (Later I realized that sex *did* play a part: because of the intimacy of our relationship, I hadn't asked/observed/discovered Richard's style the way I had with my roommates. I had *assumed*.)

I clarified my discovery a bit, then shared it with Richard. And like magic, *merely because we were aware* of the need to know, we discovered our respective styles.

We asked each other questions, we talked, we demonstrated, we fantasized. We had fun. And we learned about each other's favorite ways of entertaining. From there it was a small, simple step to developing/synthesizing our own unique *combined* style. Now, it's smooth and easy. We know the glass cabinet containing the crystal is softly lit; the lights are turned low; incense burns in discreet, strategic places; flowers are everywhere; the pottery oil lamps are lit; wine is chilled; particular munchies (tasty, healthy, rather light) are placed out in beautiful crystal dishes; and voilà! instant atmosphere! Instant party!

We are now capable of setting this up in fifteen minutes, in a pinch. We never falter, trip over each other or get irritated. Richard has his favorite responsibilities and I have mine—yet we can each cover for the other when necessary. All without much discussion.

An added bonus is, if I want Richard to feel romantic and "special occasion" without a big announcement, I can just do the "party" routine, and he's inclined to be in a party mood. *Very handy*. It's nice to have a way to let him know I think he's special that is so direct, easy and effective. If I turn on the black light in the bedroom, he also knows the mood I'm projecting. (The same is true when the roles are reversed: the messages go both ways.)

Since then, we've been conscious about style. We have developed a hot-tub style, a summer barbecue style, a traveling style, an evening-out style, a work style, etc. Actually, these styles are largely what we'd have done anyway. It's the *understanding and awareness of the style* that makes the difference.

In case this sounds rigid, I can assure you it's not. Clarity about style also makes it easy to change and communicate new ideas to each other. It's also easy to manage help when we have it, because we both know what needs to be done. Developing new styles becomes a challenge and a delightful pastime.

After seeing the impact style-consciousness made on my home life, I began to consider its implications in more profound ways. I began discussing it with friends and clients and suggesting uses of style for clients in their problem-solving processes. Everyone found it a simple and effective idea.

After getting similar positive responses in lectures and workshops, this book was conceived, in three parts: (1) a philosophical discussion of the importance of style in matters of love; (2) a series of exercises designed to help you discover your own and others' styles; and (3) a discussion, by myself and friends, of a variety of life- and lovestyles, using examples and offering options.

I hope this simple idea of styles is as profound and effective in your life as it has been in mine.

AUTHOR'S NOTE

THE INTRODUCTION has outlined the basic idea of lovestyles. The first part of this book is a philosophical discussion of the evolution and importance of lovestyles. I believe it will be useful and interesting; however, if you're reading this book looking for practical help, you may want to skip to Part Two. I know I become impatient with philosophy when I have a problem I want to solve.

Part Two is complete in its own right, so read it first if you feel in a hurry to use this information, and come back to the background in Part One later. The book is useable either way. Those of you who want understanding before experience will enjoy reading straight through. The important thing is that you begin *right now* to approach this learning process in ways that are effective for *you*.

CHAPTER ONE

LOVESTYLES

THERE'S A PERVASIVE myth in our society that there is a right and a wrong way to love. However, there's not much clarity about what the right way is. We all have difficulty with relationships, difficulty with love; therefore, we're liable to draw an uncomfortable conclusion: "Everyone knows how to love right except me." At times, when frustrated by a lover, you may indeed believe that everyone knows how to love "right" except you.

This attitude leads to blaming, defensiveness, accusing and a general shutdown of any loving feelings you *do* have. You feel helpless, betrayed, incompetent, angry and lost. You become defensive and withdraw from your beloved. It gets worse from there.

The truth is, there are as many ways of loving as there are people—and none of them is wrong. Some ways of loving do work better than others, but there are an infinite number of ways that work extremely well. This is good news, for it ends forever the fear that love can become boring, or that you can become bored with it. When looked at from this perspective, the object of relationships becomes to discover each other's way of loving (each other's lovestyle), to learn the style of loving your partner uses and to teach him/her the joys of your own style. In this way, each relationship adds to your options for love. Each new couple synthesizes a new lovestyle out of the two they bring together, one which is uniquely theirs and which can be restructured as their lifestyles change and grow.

CHAPTER TWO

LOVE

IT'S PRESUMPTUOUS OF ME to attempt to define love, for the very reasons I discussed in the introduction. So, I'm not going to define it but merely separate it from several things I believe it is *not,* and list some very general attributes of it. Please keep in mind that this is a very limited description, for the purposes of this book only. I won't presume to define what love is for you, because each of you has your own unique experience with love.

We love on many levels: romantically, practically, spiritually, familially, unconditionally, passionately, exaltedly, selfishly, etc. Here I'm talking about love at the practical level, as it's used in our day-to-day relationships.

So, accepting the above limits, what *is* love on a practical basis? Love is *my* positive experience of *you.* (I can have a positive experience of you, even when I experience your actions as negative.)

Love is universal, bringing the individual *within.*

Love is sharing and caring.

Love unites us.

Love is your willingness ot share yourself.

Love is.

Love is a state of being, a feeling, not an action. It's a warmth, a connectedness, a desire to be closer. It's my concern for your well-being, as well as my own. Love is my recognition in you of the things I like most about myself. Love is not critical or separating; it is accepting and supportive.

We hear much, especially in popular songs, movies, etc., about how painful love is. I disagree. Love doesn't hurt; whatever hurts in a relationship is not love. Love isn't limiting, it's freeing.

Love is how you feel; not what you do. The expression of love is one degree removed from the feeling itself. How you behave is not necessarily an accurate barometer of how you love—that depends on your understanding of love and your ability to express yourself effectively.

Love is a feeling; the expression of love is an art. As with any art, there can be a wide gap between what is expressed and what is felt. The difference between expression and feeling has several contributing factors: self-awareness, honesty, safety, intent and my fantasies of how you will receive my expression. As with art, practice and knowledge of technique are helpful.

COMMUNICATION AND MISCOMMUNICATION

Whether you love or not is subject only to your own opinion, no one else's. The proper answer to the age-old demand, "If you love me, you'll _____" is: "Wrong. I do love you, but I'm not going to do that," or, "I'll do that, but it's not a test of my love."

So often I've seen people let themselves be "talked right out of" loving each other. When person A says, "If you loved me, you'd _____," most often he/she is feeling insecure and asking for reassurance, but ineffectively, because it sounds like a demand. When B is also insecure, and if he/she is unwilling to do whatever is being demanded, B then tends to doubt his/her own loving: "Gee, maybe I don't love you enough. I'm not willing to do that." When A gets this doubtful response on top of his/her initially insecure feelings, A panics. "Oh no! B doesn't really love me!"

At this point, both A and B are convinced that it's not working, and everything can go downhill from there. All because of miscommunication.

Even though love is *not* a behavior but a feeling, accurate and effective communication of feelings is important. It can be very frustrating to love and be unable to communicate that love. We all know the experience of loving someone very much and having them perceive our love as something else. (Marsha: "I loved him so much, I never wanted to be away from him for a minute." Bill: "She smothered me! She had no regard for my feelings! I hated it!") Behavior contributes to accurate expression and is therefore important. It does you no good to love if your behavior is consistantly interpreted as unloving.

As in any art, it's necessary to know what you want to express in order to express it effectively. At this point, the concept of styles becomes useful.

EXPRESSIONS OF LOVE

There are many possible expressions of love:
    flowers, gifts, candy
    expensive jewelry
    touching and holding
    sexual contact
    careful listening and attention
    patience and tenderness
    phone calls, letters, cards
    cooking
    handmade things (woodworking, art, sewing, etc.)
    politeness and courtesy
    silence
    conversation
    offering companionship
    offering space
    taking out the garbage
    visiting a sickbed
    yelling
    speaking softly
    laughter
    seriousness.

You can express your love in virtually any way you can express yourself. There's no right or wrong way to express your love. What *is* important is expressing it in a way that is *understood* by your beloved.

It's important to be *effective* in your expression. What's effective varies with time, place, circumstance and the people involved. Just as your love grows and changes with time, so your expressions of love need to grow and change. The important thing is to have *options*, so that if what has worked before becomes obsolete or inappropriate, there are alternatives. Expressions of love also vary from person to person; that is, you love your spouse or lover in one way, and your various friends and family members in other ways.

CHAPTER THREE

STYLE

THE WAYS in which you express yourself are your *style* of expression. Style is individual. Style differentiates us from others. While love focuses on our connectedness, style expresses our uniqueness. As human beings, we have both a need to belong and a need to be unique. I have both a strong need to know the ways we're alike and the ways we're different. I want to know I'm accepted by my peers, yet I also want recognition for being me, for being special, for being different. These needs often appear to conflict as we search for the balance point between them.

THE "SCRIPT ONION"

Style is a combination of our belonging and our uniqueness. In order to give you a clear understanding of what style is, I'll use an illustration developed by Denton Roberts, B.Div., MFCC, called the "script onion" ("script" is a transactional analysis word describing our habitual way of being in the world, and "onion" is a description of what the picture looks like). It's a graphic representation of how we acquire our style in layers, like the layers of an onion which has been bisected.

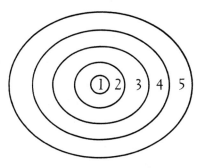

Layer 1. (Center) We are originally born unique, a special pattern of chromosomes, genes, cells, tissues, features and characteristics which are not duplicated in any other living thing, not even in identical twins. Added to that unique combination is another uniqueness, the root of what we call "personality." Paradoxically, this package contains a lot of similarities to other human beings, especially those whose genes were the instruments of our creation.

So we begin, unique and yet similar. Because we are self-aware, we recognize on a deep level the inescapable fact of our uniqueness. We also have a deep awareness of our "belonging"; we sense that we are a part of the groups surrounding us: family, friends, geographical area, race, sex, etc. The process of differentiating "self" from "other" is one of the earliest learning experiences we all face. How we accomplish it, and the conclusions we draw from it, form the first, central layer of our style.

Layer 2. (Family) Families have the same conflicting needs as the individual: to be unique and self-identified, yet part of the larger group. Families identify their uniqueness through behavior: how they celebrate holidays; how they vote; how they solve problems; how they show affection.

Sometimes the connection is made apparent through physical characteristics: almond-shaped eyes; a certain type of nose; red hair.

Although it's not often noticed, if you take a moment to remember, you can usually identify unique ways in which your family expressed love. Was your family open about loving, or silent? Was there a lot of affection, touching and hugging, or was caring shown by a loving look, a small considerate gesture? Remember what it was like as a small child to go to another family for a visit; recall the differences between your family and theirs. Pay attention to your family's *style*.

A good beginning is to contrast styles of holiday observations. I became acutely aware of style differences during my experience of living together cooperatively with six other adults and two children—we all moved in together on Labor Day weekend, early in September.

As we settled in and approached the end of October, Riley (my good friend and co-author) said at our house meeting that he was nervous about the coming holidays. He was recently divorced and had had a difficult time the first Christmas after he was married because he and his new wife couldn't agree on Christmas customs. So he thought that with nine people (four families), the holidays were going to get out of hand for us.

Thus forewarned, we began to discuss it and found that we did indeed have widely different styles regarding holidays. The discussions got quite heated before we reached a cooperative solution. However, we did eventually find one, and the result was the most wonderful and memorable

Thanksgiving and Christmas I had ever had. Bringing all those separate and unique styles together to synthesize something new created a wonderfully rich and varied celebration.

For example, each of us wanted to spend Thanksgiving together with our "new family," yet we all had our existing families to consider. Solution: We invited everyone to join us, and made the dinner a potluck. Instead of the pleasant but somewhat boring traditional family dinners we had all had before, we created an exciting party for about thirty-five people. No one had to work too hard, everyone got to participate, and we didn't end the party until 3:00 A.M.

Our house was big enough so that each of us had our own "suite" of rooms; when we wanted to be private with our own relatives or friends, that was easty, too. Since then, all my Thanksgivings have been potluck and have included any friends who wanted to join in. It's always a great day!

Our Christmas solutions were equally successful. The first disagreement was about the tree. Sentimentalists wanted the smell of a fresh tree; conservationists wanted an artificial one, to preserve the forests. Solution: We organized an expedition to a local tree farm near the freeway and cut our own, thereby not endangering the forest, yet having a fresh tree.

Some people wanted to open presents on Christmas Eve, and some wanted Santa Claus to come at night so they could open presents in the morning. Solution: We each selected a present to open Christmas Eve, and Christmas morning someone dressed up as Santa, and the two children dressed as elves, and they passed out all the presents.

We had breakfast together, then scattered to various families to have dinner.

This same enrichment and variety is possible whenever we bring two or more styles together. If we can drop our focus on right and wrong and just weigh options, our solutions become better than the original traditions.

One more reminiscence about Christmas: Several of us had decorations which had been traditional to us and had great sentimental value. We decided to cull through our individual collections and choose the ones that were most important, having agreed that we would use all the ones chosen.

The result: We decorated the house and tree together on a Saturday and finished just at sunset. When we plugged in the lights on the decorated tree, we spontaneously joined hands around it and burst into carols and tears all at the same time. It is a moment I will never forget, and it illustrates the result of sharing and including everyone's wishes.

Layer 3. (Neighborhood) The next layer out from family is the neighborhood, town or village—the small geographical area surrounding the family. I come from a small upstate New York farm community. There was a rivalry between my town and the next one, especially in high school; even a rivalry between one school class and another. There was the dichotomy of identification with the group versus the need to be unique. In my high school we were rivals, class-to-class and club-to-club, but we banded together in differentiating ourselves from other schools. In our attempts to become identified with the larger group, we absorb more style options and learn new ways of self-expression. In our attempts to be unique, we adapt and modify these new options to make them ours; and we become more clearly aware of our differences—our own style.

Layer 4 and beyond: Beyond neighborhood, class or group the layers move outward: county, state, geographic area, nationality, race, gender. Each layer has aspects we wish to separate ourselves from and aspects we wish to be identified with. Some are more important to us than others. From each layer we pick up style options, or ways of self-expression. When someday earth makes contact with other intelligent life forms, we'll add one more layer: species.

OPTIONS AND CHOICES

All these layers upon layers of experience and identity become the source of all our options. From these options we choose, consciously and unconsciously, those modes of thought and behavior which become our means of self-expression—our style.

It's important to note that these choices are not always voluntary. They may be heavily reinforced by traumatic life experiences; by group or peer pressure to conform/rebel; by our own correct or mistaken impressions that we must adopt some style elements in order to survive.

Jim and Julie (not their real names) came to me to resolve their domestic battles about housekeeping. They were afraid they would have to get a divorce. Jim was the son of an alcoholic mother; he developed the habit of going to his room immediately upon getting home from school. If his bed was made, he was OK; if not, Mom would be drunk and dangerous.

Currently, Jim and Julie were having terrible fights about her occasional lapses in bedmaking. If she forgot, or was in a rush and neglected making the bed, he treated it as though she had done him a terrible injury. She couldn't understand his "unreasonable overreaction" until she learned the origin of this peculiar lifestyle.

Jim couldn't remember why a neatly made bed was so important; he simply couldn't control his reaction. Learning that this aspect of his style had been acquired involuntarily, as a survival aid, made it possible for him to gain control of it and to dissociate unmade beds from disaster.

Understanding this involuntary response gave Jim and Julie the ability to solve their problem. They began to make the bed together, ritually, every morning. This changed the emotional atmosphere and made it very easy for Jim to relax. Julie got to feel special for being loving and understanding and to feel she was contributing to Jim's emotional well-being as well as to the health of their relationship.

CHANGING STYLES

Style is both the way in which you communicate to others and the way in which you identify yourself as you. Its origin is in your experiences and observations as you live your life. Some aspects of style are heavily ingrained, either because they were learned very early and are thus hard to differentiate, or because they were heavily reinforced by a traumatic or pressurizing circumstance. All aspects of style, whether acquired voluntarily and consciously or involuntarily and unconsciously, can be changed. Indeed, you change styles quite often, as different needs arise in life, or as you observe an unfamiliar and attractive new style option and decide to adopt it.

I, Tina, think of myself as:
    human
    woman
    Italian/American
    Protestant
    educated
    now living on the West Coast
    originally from the Northeast
    a city dweller
    originally from the country
    a Bellocchio (maiden name)
    Mrs. Richard Sharrard (current marriage)
    a member of my "chosen family" (my longtime intimate friends)
    an only child
    a unique spark of life which has never before been on this planet.

All these self-given labels have history and meaning for me, and I express myself through the options I experienced at each level. I'm concerned for all people because I'm one of them (human); I'm aware of women's issues a bit more than I might be as a man; I'm overtly emotional and expressive because of my Italian heritage; I'm concerned with personal rights and freedom because I am an American; and so on.

Some of my historical options didn't work very well for me, so I chose new ones. As I encountered others whose ways worked better than my own, I "borrowed" new ways of expressing myself. I customized these options as I adopted them, to make them fit me better and better express my true feelings.

There are components of my personal style that I cherish, but I have learned to modify even some of those. For example: I grew up in an Italian restaurant and I know Italian cooking well. I enjoy both cooking and eating the result. As my knowledge of health and diet has increased, I've learned to alter my cooking style: I use less fat and more whole foods; I pick recipes which are lighter and healthier; and I modify those that aren't. Now I still get to enjoy my favorite foods, but without worrying about damaging my body.

YOU'RE IN CONTROL

So it is with all aspects of style. *You* are the one in control, no matter how thorough your early training; no matter how ingrained your self-definitions and habits. You can observe your own style, amplify those aspects you enjoy and that work well for you and modify those that don't.

To clients who tell me they "can't control" themselves when they're angry or afraid, I always respond with the same metaphor: Suppose you were in your VW bug, driving on the freeway, and a big semi cut you off and moved into your lane. If you're like most people, not wishing to destroy yourself, you'd control your anger and assure your safety by moving out of the way. Later, you might "blow off steam" by talking to your friends or punching a pillow.

Controlling your feelings in your relationship utilizes the same technique. If you *know* that a particular response of anger or fear will seriously damage your relationship (and let's face it, you almost always do), why make it? Leave the room, take a break, talk to a friend or counselor—but don't destroy your relationship out of immediate gratification and self-indulgence. That's a heavy price to pay for not taking responsibility for the expression of your feelings.

I think of this acceptance of responsibility for yourself and your choices as being a "grown-up" in relationships. To move your interaction from a "stuck" (angry, frustrated, stubborn) place requires at least one person able to think and make choices.

While we all have an "inner-child" aspect which we must love and respect, we do not benefit from allowing that part of us to control our lives. If you need a childlike outburst for relief, either be sure your partner's willing to take the "grown-up" role while you do it, *or* find someone else (perhaps a therapist, friend or relative) who will, *or* go off and be alone for a while to blow off steam. When you feel like a "grown-up" again, you can effectively deal with your partner.

If outbursts are a common part of your relationship and you feel unable to control them, here's a suggestion from *Learning to Live Without Violence*, an excellent book written for men, but equally useable by women:

> Whenever you feel your anger rising, your body getting tense like it is going to explode, or you begin to feel frustrated or out of control, say out loud to yourself and your wife or lover: "I'm beginning to feel angry and I need to take a Time-Out."

You must leave your home for one hour (no longer and no shorter), during which you *cannot* drink and you should *not* drive (unless it is absolutely necessary). It is most preferable for you to go for a walk or run, to do something physical. If you begin to think about the situation that made you feel angry, just say to yourself: "I'm beginning to feel angry and I need to take a Time-Out." In this way you will be taking a mental Time-Out as well as a physical Time-Out.

When you return in one hour, check in and tell your partner that you have come back from your Time-Out and ask if she would like to talk with you. If you *both* want to discuss the situation, tell her what it was that made you angry. You may also want to talk about what it was like for you to take a Time-Out.

If one of you doesn't want to talk about the situation, respect that person's need to not discuss it. In either case, if you find yourself feeling angry again, take another Time-Out.

Some topics of conversation may be too charged to talk about. If this is true in your situation, put that issue on the shelf for a while, acknowledging that it is too difficult for the two of you to discuss alone. Take these issues and others to a counselor to get some help working them out. Even if it's an important issue, think of your priorities. Nothing can be more important than stopping the violence!

. . . When there has been violence in a relationship, the trust factor drops significantly. This Time-Out exercise not only helps to stop the violence, but also helps to rebuild trust. Trust takes some time to rebuild. Just because you may take one or two Time-Outs, it doesn't mean that everything is OK. Be patient! Concentrate on identifying your anger and taking your Time-Outs. The rest takes time. (Sonkin and Durphy [Volcano Press, 1982].)

The authors go on to say that "practice Time-Outs" (taken when there's no problem), like any practice, make it much easier and much more likely that you'll be able to take real Time-Outs when you need to. This is a book I recommend highly to *anyone* who's been involved in domestic violence. Although written for the heterosexual male, it offers sound advice to anyone who needs alternatives to physical and/or verbal violence.

ALTERING YOUR STYLE

Because style is *behavior* and not your actual emotions, you can alter it. Usually, the alterations are quite minor, yet they produce major results in terms of personal satisfaction and effectiveness with others.

The essence of *yourself*—how you're *feeling*; your *reactions* to whatever life offers you; your *desires* to affect your environment—that essence is always filtered through your style—how you've learned to behave in your environment and your perceptions of what events in that environment mean.

Many clients who come to me for change are afraid that they'll lose "who they are" in the process. Therefore they've only decided to seek change because their fear of what's currently happening in their lives is greater than their fear of loss of identity.

What is happening in their lives, then, is *crisis*—a drastic state of affairs which has frightened them severely. In relationships, this often means a break-up or divorce. When clients find out how simple the necessary changes are, and that they will still recognize themselves, they're often angry that it took so long for them to get ready to change.

However, although simple, change is not necessarily *easy*, because they're changing ingrained habits of communication, long-standing perceptions and their view of what events mean to them.

Stan Dale, in his "What is Sex?" workshops, effectively explains these changes with the following exercise: Hold your hands in front of you and clasp them together, palms facing, fingers intertwined. Now look at your hands. Which thumb is on top, the right or the left? You'll find that whichever thumb it is, you *always* clasp your hands together the same way, with the same thumb on top.

Now, clasp your hands together the *opposite* way, fingers on the other side, with the other thumb on top. Pay attention to how "wrong" it feels—how out of place each finger feels. Stan explains that we have "neuronal pathways" in our brains which have developed to make habitual activities automatic—that is, we do them the same way every time, according to the pattern we've developed. When we do something different, against the "neuronal pathways," we feel uncomfortable until new pathways are created.

This type of change requires repetition—just as the original learning required repeated experiences—and it requires *awareness*, being alert so that we don't slip back into unconscious "old behavior." However, the changes seldom need to be very drastic or dramatic. A minor alteration of style can have a major effect on the outcome.

For example, if one partner is used to a family style in which everyone talks simultaneously, and the other is used to quiet politeness, merely having the first partner insert spaces in his/her patter can allow both an equal opportunity to talk.

This changing process is uncomfortable, like putting your hands together in a new way is uncomfortable. However, in a short time the new pathways are developed, the new habit is formed and the discomfort is gone. It's worth "hanging in there" with the discomfort of change, since change can never be as difficult as continuing behavior that doesn't work in your life.

CHAPTER FOUR

COMMUNICATION

HOW DO WE ARRIVE AT such simple solutions? Communication is necessary. We can't arrive at a solution before we understand the problem, and understanding both sides of the difficulty is essential in problems involving two people.

Because we acquire style in such an unconscious, gradual way, because it's learned as a result of our experience in the environment, it's difficult to realize that style even *exists*. Becoming aware of style, that everyone has a style and that everyone's style is unique, can be a life-changing bit of truth. In regard to relationships and communication, even just the *awareness* that style exists can be dramatically effective. Here's an example of the effectiveness of style awareness:

THE DISASTER EQUATION

There's a common relationship occurrence which I call the "Disaster Equation." I can explain it like this:

(A loves B the way A wants to be loved) +
(B loves A the way B wants to be loved) =

(A feels unloved and unappreciated for loving) +
(B feels unloved and unappreciated for loving).

The resentment builds on both sides; a natural disaster with mutual accusations and mutual guilt is the result.

But if both A and B realize that lovestyles are unique and that A may not understand how B loves, and vice versa; then assumptions underlying the original equation change as follows:

A & B now approach each other in a learning/teaching mode.

A learns how B wants to be loved; teaches B how to love A.

B learns how A wants to be loved; teaches A how to love B.

Then:

(A loves B the way B wants to be loved) +
(new ways B has learned to understand and appreciate) +
(B loves A the way A wants to be loved) +
(new options A has learned to like) =

(A feels loved; appreciated for loving and excited about new discoveries) +

(B feels loved, appreciated for loving and excited about new discoveries.)

This all comes about because A and B have recognized the necessity of learning and teaching styles. They dropped their assumptions about the meanings of each other's behavior and learned to question and understand each other. It really is that simple.

The hard part is remembering how simple it is when things get tense, angry or scary.

SOLVING PROBLEMS IS SIMPLE

Here's how I remember how simple it is:

I have a personal belief that there is a purpose to every circumstance of my life, that I am here to *learn*. The result of this belief is that problems have become exercises in learning, puzzles to solve. From that perspective, there's very little to fear. It's not a matter of one false move and I'm lost forever; it's a matter of attempting various ways of solving the problem until I finally succeed.

I put it this way in a magazine article:

SIGNING UP FOR THE COURSE

We are all quite practiced in taking courses. When we sign up for an algebra course, for example, we know what we face: ten (or so) weeks of learning new material and homework assignments consisting of more and more complex problems based on the material we have learned. We may grumble about the homework load, or complain about the teacher, but we never think we've been given the problems because we are bad people. The problems are a natural facet of the educational process.

Life, too, is a classroom with many classes. The signing-up process has become rather subtle and mysterious, so we have a tendency to forget what we are doing. I have found that by keeping in mind I am a student, and problems are for learning, life is much easier, growth is faster, and everything now makes sense.

How can you look at relationships as courses in personal growth?

Begin by re-evaluating the purpose of your relationships. Use them as a training ground. Assume there will be a lot to learn, and lots of problems to solve, which increase in complexity as you gain in knowledge. Never, ever, do the problems indicate that you deserve punishment, or that you did something bad. They only show that you have something to learn, and even give you the means to learn it. A problem does not exist without a valuable lesson attached.

Just as in school, if you do not understand the lesson and solve the problem, you will keep getting it back in altered forms, until you do understand. This is *not* to give you a hard time, but to teach you something you must know to live a fuller, more loving life.

Doing Your Homework

So, when problems arise, stop a moment and think before you react with outrage and hurt. Say to yourself, "What was I given this problem for? What can I learn from this/ What do I need to know to solve it?" View the problem as a homework assignment, and figure out what it has been designed to teach you. ("Your Relationship: A Course in Spiritual Growth," *Magical Blend* No. 10, c1983.)

COMMUNICATION AND LEARNING

I see communication and learning as the major function of relationships. That is, when we look back from the perspective of history, what seem important and what stand out as the major memorable events in our lives turn out to be the lessons we learned and the times we felt understood and understanding (communication).

In communication, compatibility of style is crucial. That is, if my communication style is to speak English, and yours is to speak Greek, we're going to have difficulty communicating. That seems absurdly obvious. However, if my style is quite nonverbal, and yours is very word-oriented, we could have a problem as difficult as different languages, complicated by the fact that *we cannot easily see what the problem is*. Because the style of our communication is so important, it becomes important to understand style differences.

We live in an efficient age. Computers, mass media, travel, have all contributed to making our communication more efficient (though not necessarily more *effective*). Therefore, it seems logical that we should desire efficient and effective communication in our personal lives also.

How often have I heard in my counseling office, "I just want to be understood!" (How often have I said it myself!) Interestingly enough, I frequently find that when an angry marital partner finally feels understood by his/her mate, the anger subsides. Often, yelling and fighting is an attempt to be heard. When you feel ignored or misunderstood, you're apt to boost the volume, the way people sometimes shout at a person who speaks another language, as though it'll help them be understood. For people who are not comfortable with anger and fighting, crying can be an attempt to be heard. Stony silence can indicate hopelessness about ever being heard or understood. Good communication skills can clear up many of these relationship hassles.

Often it's easier to solve a problem than to understand it. When dealing with couples in difficulty who think their relationship is in a serious condition, I frequently find that one session of helping them hear and understand each other convinces them that the relationship is not as much of a problem as they thought.

Communication expands options. When you understand what the problem is and hear both sides of it, you immediately have more choice. Getting out of the struggle and into listening and learning gives you not only your own idea of what the problem is and what might solve it, but also your partner's ideas. With this expanded number of choices, the solution often becomes obvious.

CHAPTER FIVE

SYNTHESIS

THE OBJECTIVE OF ALL this understanding, awareness and communication is *synthesis*—the blending of two styles into a new, expanded style that includes enough options for both individuals to freely express themselves *without constantly having to explain.*

This concept came as a shock to me. I believe I first realized it in teaching. When I began teaching subjects familiar to me for a long time, I experienced difficulty in communicating with my students. It quickly came to my attention that I was speaking a kind of "expert shorthand" or "jargon" that my students didn't know.

This knowledge was so much a part of my thinking that I *couldn't remember what it was like not to know it!* I had to struggle to think at a level "before learning" in order to be able to communicate with people thinking at that level, and of course, in order to teach.

All the teachers I know to whom I have spoken about this situation experienced that same problem at first. Adults who spend time with small children (such as parents and teachers) are keenly aware of it. It requires special thought and effort to communicate with someone who doesn't yet understand what "near and far" means.

Once this difference in understanding is recognized, it becomes a very effective teaching tool, and those beloved teachers who have lit up our lives from time to time are masters at communicating on the level of our current understanding.

KNOWLEDGE COMPRESSION

What this all means is that as our knowledge grows through living and learning, we *compress* it into more efficient packages. Get together with scientists, computer programmers or graduates of an esoteric course like EST, and they sound incomprehensible to an outsider.

In fact, get together as an outsider with a group of long-time friends, and the same thing happens. "Remember Graduation Day?" is a phrase which efficiently compresses hundreds of shared bits of memory into only three words. If you weren't present at "Graduation Day," you're left out.

This compression of knowledge into "jargon" or "reminiscences" happens naturally, a mysterious function of our magical minds. However, you can use this natural occurrence consciously and to your advantage. That's what synthesis (in my terms, for the purpose of this book) is all about.

Please note that we're accomplishing this already. "Lovestyles" and "synthesis" are two of several terms you've already acquired which compress the knowledge of this book. *But these words are only useful to yourself and others who are reading this book,* even though the concepts can be understood by anyone.

If you search your own experience, you'll be able to come up with many areas of knowledge that have been compressed into jargon. With intimate friends, "special" words or phrases have certain meanings.

I once gave Richard a greeting card which said "I Love You" all over the front cover. Inside, it said, "It's a dirty job, but someone has to do it." That card was my way of telling him that a difficult situation we had just experienced had not affected my love. Since then, we've often said, "It's a dirty job . . ." to each other, and we laugh. At that minute, we're both flooded by warm, affectionate feelings and reminded that we share important history. That same phrase can be used as shorthand when we're around others who don't understand what we mean.

Some gay men friends of mine who are musicians use "1–4–3," spoken or written, to say "I love you" when circumstances make it awkward to be open. The numbers correspond to the number of letters in the words. They also happen to symbolize musical chords, in the universal language of music. My friends can also choose to play the corresponding musical chords, instead of using the numbers. Because of their training, they instantly recognize the chord sequence and have communicated wordlessly. It's very efficient and extremely handy. This is a positive and effective use of condensed ideas.

In a relationship, "jargon" or "code words" can be symbolic of synthesis. The more you learn about each other, the more history you share, the more likely you are to have "special" words and phrases known only to the two of you. With these handy little timesavers, you can say a great deal in a short time. In addition to that benefit, you can also pinpoint a shared meaning. That is, when you speak a catch phrase like "1–4–3," you know *accurately* what your partner hears, because you've worked it out in advance.

USING SYNTHESIS

Synthesis, then, becomes the process of taking your separate and varied experiences and ideas, *examining* them, *sharing* them and *combining* them into a whole that is more than the sum of its parts, because you've added mutual understanding.

An example of synthesis: Remember my story about giving parties with Richard? Here's how the synthesis looks: I had been used to parties where there were lots of candles; where carefully prepared food was important; where there were fresh flowers; where music was an important part of the evening; where there were several rooms available, so people could play music, talk, smoke or be outside as they wished.

Richard's experience had been simpler: more bring-your-own type food; less formal; some games, such as *Trivial Pursuit*; a smaller space, because he had been living in an apartment until we moved to our house.

Our party synthesis has all these elements: the bring-your-own idea sounded great to me (a lot less work), so we usually have pot-luck hors d'oeuvres; one of the extra rooms is set up for games, etc; candles were too messy for Richard, so he introduced me to the elegant oil lamps now available, and we have those; the patio is nicely lit with candles for the smokers. Both of us often bring home flowers before a party.

Everything that was important to either of us is included, and we're very happy with the result.

Here's an example of synthesis arising out of family tradition differences:

Shortly after we were married, Richard left for his first business trip since we'd met. Now in my big, noisy Italian family, the occasion of a departure was *really* an occasion! Even if you were only going for one day, the whole family trooped out to your car or train or whatever, and everyone cried. They said: "We'll miss you" in a hundred ways; and if they *didn't* do that, something was terribly wrong!

Richard, on the other hand, comes from a Midwestern family that avoids good-byes. If you're going away for a long time, or on a big trip, they have a family gathering the evening before you leave, and that serves as your farewell. When you actually leave, they politely disappear, to save you the discomfort of saying good-bye.

So, there we were: Richard with suitcase in hand, me with handkerchief (unconsciously attempting to make up for the absence of a large family). I started to weep and said, "I don't know what I'm going to do without you" (remember, I'm usually a very independent woman). I was shocked as Richard got angry: "What's the matter? Don't you want me to have a good time?"

I realized we had a miscommunication somewhere, so, because he had to leave, I pulled myself together, smiled and said, "Of course I do. Have a wonderful time. I'll be fine." And he left. When he came back, we talked about it. I described my family ritual to him, and he described his. He came to call my tearful emotional outbursts "Italian Celebrations."

Six months later, we had been struggling with another problem for about a week and had finally solved it. I came in from my office on the day we resolved our struggle, and there was a giant heart drawn with a white cord on our king-size bed. It was Richard's way of saying, "I love you. I'm glad it's over."

I, of course, started to cry. I called him at work, sobbing, and said through my tears, "That's beautiful!" His response was, "What's the matter? Are you hurt? Are the dogs OK?" (He still thinks tears mean tragedy.) I said, "No (sniff, sniff), I'm happy!" He paused, then said (suspiciously), "Is this an Italian Celebration?" When I said yes, we started to talk about how happy we were, and he got teary-eyed too! He had a new option for expression.

The day I left to sign the contract for this book, Richard knew it was a big occasion for me, so he stood at the door until I was out of sight and actually waved a handkerchief! It was one of the most loving moments I've ever experienced, because I felt loved, cared about, accepted and understood all at once. He actualy went out of his way to say good-bye in *my* style!

As it now stands, we've learned a lot from each other, and we continue to learn. Best of all, neither one of us feels as though the other is "trying to change me." The changes are voluntary, because we know a good idea when we see one, and because we're not locked in a right-wrong struggle.

Honestly, as wonderful as our relationship is, we *do* still get into right-wrong struggles, and when we do, we resent each other. The important thing is that we realize it *doesn't work* with resentment, and we always come around to learning from each other eventually. Only from that learning space do we actually get anywhere with the problem, whatever it is.

It doesn't do me any good to label Richard "cold" and insist that he learn to cry. He doesn't get anywhere by calling me "too emotional." It's only when we *understand* our emotional style differences that we can deal with them, and in the atmosphere of understanding and acceptance we're both open to learning from each other. So Richard learns to express himself more emotionally and I learn to think more rationally, which gets both of us more understanding.

YOU ALREADY KNOW HOW TO LOVE

I'm not talking here about *how* to love. In your own awareness, you already know that. Love is such a unique, individual, creative process, I wouldn't know how to begin to tell you how. My objective is to help you expand your options for expression, and to help you communicate your love more effectively. Also, one of the "magic" things about this information is that when you learn to love more effectively, you also learn to *be loved* more effectively.

It's possible to learn to have a workable relationship with *anyone*, no matter how different your lovestyles are. However, it's important to note that the greater the difference, the more energy it takes to work it out. This is fine for people who have decided that relationships are a central aspect of their lives, as I have, and who are content to spend a lot of energy on them.

But for those of you who want your relationship to be a "haven" from the hassles of the other aspects of living, for those who want to devote most of their energy to career or children or artistic endeavors, it's wise to select a mate whose lovestyle is very much like your own, or someone who's willing to do most of the learning and growing (as far as the relationship goes).

Even if you do choose to work it out with someone very different from yourself, it's essential that you have some support from others who "do it your way." It gets frustrating and can be hard on your self-confidence to be always in the presence of someone who "sees it differently." You can begin to doubt yourself and start believing in the old right/wrong way again. A break from the relationship with a friend who "does it your way" can renew your energy for learning, just as vacation breaks can renew your energy for school or work.

Please don't get the impression that I'm promoting only "unusual" or alternative relationships. I'm merely saying that *any* lovestyle/lifestyle *can* work, with the proper information and processing. Whether you want lots of difference or lots of similarity is a matter of preference.

TRAINING EACH OTHER

One of the aspect of synthesis that can *create* problems in a relationship is what I call "training each other." Because we care, because human beings are born sensitive to the responses of those about them, we cannot avoid unconsciously (as well as consciously) affecting each others' behavior. Without conscious thought, we all learn quickly what gets "results" with the people we spend time with.

The most outstanding example of this I've seen was a married couple who came to me for counseling, feeling upset and hopeless about their relationship. I'll call them Ivy and Rock. Rock was angry: "Ivy was so soft-spoken when I married her—she never raised her voice. Now she sounds just like my first wife, who is a shrew!" After considerable discussion with both of them over a few sessions, the reason for Ivy's change became obvious.

According to Ivy, "We have never been late paying the first wife's child support, but she still calls and screams at Rock. When she does, he'll do anything to get rid of her, including paying child support before it's due, and using up all our grocery money to do it! Then I have to struggle to feed us and the children until he gets paid again! When I protest, he doesn't want to hear it, until I'm so desperate and so angry, I lose control and start screaming."

Neither Rock nor Ivy saw the connection between these two things, but it was clear from my perspective (it's often easier to see clearly when you're not emotionally involved) that Rock was "training" Ivy to scream, because the "screamer" got the rewards from him. Willing to do anything to avoid a scene, he didn't think about anything but the immediate situation. So, Ivy's only choice (she felt) was to become the loudest screamer.

Rock looked like he'd been hit between the eyes when he understood this. "You mean I 'trained' my first wife to be a screamer, too?"

I said, "It's possible she already had a tendency to yell, but by giving in, you probably encouraged her. At any rate, it's as easy to train a person to learn that yelling *doesn't* work with you, so rather than worry about the past, let's correct the present."

Rock then practiced other responses to yelling, such as saying, "I can't hear you when you do that. Call me back when you can talk calmly," and hanging up the phone. Or, "I'm not going to give you anything when you yell at me. If you want something different from our legal agreement, let's discuss it calmly, and I'll see what I can do to help."

Ivy also agreed to help by remaining calm and warning Rock when she felt like yelling, instead of actually yelling. It took time for Rock to learn to make the new responses, and more time for the first wife to be "retrained," but it did work, and he now has calmer, more thoughtful problem-solving sessions with both his current wife and the former one. Ivy and Rock feel much better about their marriage, and they are both aware now of how they "train" each other unintentionally, so they work on consciously correcting their counterproductive habits.

Just as we can teach each other to bring flowers on special occasions, we can also teach undesirable responses. Simple awareness of this helps to change the dynamics.

Many people complain to me that their beloved never calls them or asks them out or shows any initiative or enthusiasm about seeing them. This happens both in longterm relationships and in brand-new ones. Very frequently I find they have unconsciously created this situation themselves.

Each of us has a slightly different "rhythm" about making contact. If you get together with someone whose pace is just a bit slower than yours, you're inclined to create the above situation, "training" the other person *not* to call you or show initiative. If you think a call every day is perfect, but your partner likes to call every other day, then you may keep calling before he/she ever gets the urge. After a little while, your partner gives up calling because it's not necessary, and he/she may even be feeling a little badgered by your daily calls.

In your partner's unconscious thought, you begin to lose value, because you're too "available" or "easy" to contact.

Your partner never gets a chance to think, "Gee, I'd like to hear X's voice." He/she is more likely to think, "Oh, it's X again," and even try to avoid talking to you. He/she may be puzzled about that reluctance to talk to you, or even feel guilty about it, and begin to find "excuses" for why you aren't exciting to him/her anymore.

Before this gets too scary, let me say it's easily solved. Just back off! If you feel neglected, or feel that you're doing more than your share, put your energy somewhere else for a while and give your partner time to miss you. This works so well, you won't believe it! The hard part will be getting yourself to back off. Your too-fast pattern may have evolved out of an inner insecurity you aren't aware of, and you may wind up facing that when you don't call your beloved for a few days.

Remember, your partner has developed a habit of leaving it "all up to you," so it'll take a while for the reality that you *really aren't going to call* to sink in. And it'll take even longer than that for him/her to decide to call you to find out why. But he/she *will call*. I can guarantee that if you just wait long enough, and if there is any relationship there at all, you *will* get a call. Then you get to discover your partner's love-style, in terms of how often he/she wants contact. Once you know that, you can work out a synthesis that's right for you both.

In general, if you remember that we're always learning from each other and adding to the layers of our "onion," you can be more aware of your own effect on those around you. Pay attention to how you're responding to others, and to what you're rewarding with your own responses. Ask yourself, "Is this response going to get me what I want, or is it going to work against me?"

Remember that no one else can be controlled. You cannot force or coerce your beloved to do what you would like. But you can *allow* him/her to do it by making it the *most attractive* or most *well-rewarded* option available. In that way, you're cooperating together to design a lovestyle that works for both of you.

Sometimes, when people have heard the foregoing information, they've decided I'm talking about "brainwashing" or "manipulating" others. I definitely am not. What I am doing is pointing out that our behavior toward other people causes responses from them. We can observe our own behavior and the responses we get from others; then, by controlling our own behavior, we can invite desirable responses from others.

The other people still get to choose their responses. Since these are people who care about you, they're as eager to build relationships that work well as you are. Their responses will naturally be intended to produce loving feelings in you, especialy if you make that easy.

Stop and think a moment. Haven't you, in a fit of anger, occasionally said things that were *calculated* to hurt or anger someone? Of course, you have—we all have. Well, if you can do that, why can't you choose to say things that are calculated to be effective in creating more love for both of you?

A bright "Hi, how are you?" with a smile is a lot more likely to get a good response than a sarcastic "Oh. It's only you." We all know that, and we use it, if we're smart. It's OK to be intelligent about love, too. It's one of the ways you can learn to be a "grown-up" in your relationship.

A brief digression: I frequently get angry at the experts who want to tell me *how* to love. My anger comes from my experience with numerous clients who believe that someone outside them can tell them how to love, but that they can't do it "right" by themselves. This only propagates the "myth" that there *is* a "right" way to love.

Love is an intangible, subject to personal opinion, and there is *no right or wrong way*. There is only what works and what doesn't. The final judge of whether you're loving or not is *you. Do you feel loved? Do you feel loving?* Ask yourself those questions enough times and you'll teach yourself how to love.

The objective of all this discussion is to increase your options. This book is about options, how to discover them and how to offer new options to those you love (including yourself).

I hope that after you've read this book completely, you'll find you have many more options than when you began. Even better, you'll have methods for discovering new options you can use for the rest of your life. So, if you feel up to it, write and let me know whether I've achieved my goal of effectively giving you useful information about new options for expressing love and understanding love that's expressed to you.

Write to: Tina B. Tessina
             P.O. Box 4883
             Long Beach, CA 90804–4883

Thanks.

EXERCISES

INTRODUCTION

How to use this section: The exercises contained in this part of the book are divided into three types: (1) those which will probably be most valuable to singles and to people wishing to create a new relationship and seeking information on finding people with compatible lovestyles; also readers who already have partners but are reading the book on their own; (2) those most valuable to people just beginning a new relationship and who want to lay a firm foundation; and (3) those most useful to people who already have an ongoing, longterm relationship but who want to correct difficulties and enhance what they have.

It's important that you remember these divisions are arbitrary. I've organized the exercises in a framework which seems viable and effective in general. Read through all of them and customize them to suit yourself and your situation. Each section of exercises includes versions to be done alone and versions to be done with a partner. The partner may be lover, spouse or a friend who wants to become familiar with lovestyles.

For those of you in multiple relationships, all the exercises intended for New Relationships and Longterm Relationships can be done by more than two people. In the dialogues, just go clockwise around a circle of however many you are, and the person on your left responds as your "partner," gives his/her response, and so on.

It's not necessary for your significant partner to participate in order for this information to be useful and effective in your relationship. Please save yourself stress and don't attempt to pressure an unwilling person to join you. The exercises are very useful done alone and far more effective than anything done with a reluctant (and possibly resentful) partner.

If the number of exercises seems overwhelming to you, just pick one that seems to fit your life and try it out. I'm probably providing more than you need because I believe that the more options we have available, the better. There is a brief explanation of the focus of the exercises in each section.

Also, feel free to try the exercises in the sections suggested for people in other situations. There's nothing here that can hurt you—this is merely a process of self-discovery and consciousness-raising. The sections are merely to help organize the material, not to restrict your freedom.

The only way you can get into difficulty is by pressuring yourself or someone else into using this book or doing the exercises. That's emotionally equivalent to beating yourself or someone else with the book, and that is not its intent.

You'll be taking some risks here. Even if you're alone when you do these exercises, you risk challenging some of your precious beliefs about yourself and your relationships. If you're doing these with a partner, your risk increases. So go gently. If you're doing the exercises and you wind up angry, frustrated or fighting with each other, you've misunderstood the intent of the instructions. In that case, these may not be appropriate exercises for you at this stage in your life.

No book can provide a safe, supportive atmosphere by itself. You must be prepared to do that yourself, or to get some professional help. Calm down, find a way to heal whatever has gotten hurt and leave these exercises for another time. If you are a couple, try doing the "singles" exercises separately for a while, and see if they work better for you.

If you wind up bemused, full of new insight, excited about what you're learning and feeling that you have new options, then this book is perfect for you now. Please do what you will with these exercises—stretch them, bend them, tailor them to your heart's desire. If you get a new idea or two about some aspect of life and love from merely reading them, they will have amply fulfilled their purpose.

NOTE FOR PROFESSIONALS

I hope you will find this book an excellent resource for your classes, workshops and therapy sessions. However, please carefully consider the people with whom you are working and adjust the exercises accordingly. You have the joy of knowing your clients and students personally and can therefore be much more effective than I can, who must try to anticipate the needs of unknown readers.

If you do use these exercises, I would appreciate a mention of this book, and my publisher will be happy to give you a discount if you decide to buy the book in quantity for your students or clients. Feedback on your success with this information would also be useful. Thank you.

CHAPTER ONE

DEFINING AND DISCOVERING YOUR OWN LOVESTYLE

THE IMPORTANCE OF recognizing and defining your own lovestyle becomes clear when you realize that you must be able to understand anything you wish to communicate. In my counseling experience, I have frequently been amazed to discover how often people don't realize that they *already have what they want*, because they have never really defined it. When you're not clear on what your goal is, it can slide right past you without being seen.

Many times when I've helped someone clearly define what he/she wants, my client suddenly realizes that many of his/her desires have already been achieved, and that the problem lies only in one small area which can be corrected or restructured with minimal effort. We all seem to have a tendency to generalize, feeling that everything is a mess whenever one minor aspect goes haywire.

Not long ago, Richard pointed out to me that every time we had a disagreement, we spoke as though *everything* between us was bad. We agreed at that point to make more of the good times, marking all the good days on our calendar, so we wouldn't forget. That process was very reassuring and made our small problems seem less important and less threatening. Everything suddenly gained perspective.

Similarly, when we were arguing about whether we were devoting sufficient time to each other and our relationship, our counselor suggested we mark that time on our calendar for a couple of weeks, to check the reality of our individual assertions about time. We both learned a lot from that one!

Knowing what it takes to be satisfied, knowing what you want and then recognizing it whenever you get it, are the preliminary steps to finding or building a relationship that works for you.

NOTE: PLEASE REMEMBER TO MAKE THIS EASY ON YOURSELF. DO ONLY ONE EXERCISE AT A TIME, AND GIVE YOURSELF A CHANCE TO THINK ABOUT YOUR REACTIONS TO IT IN BETWEEN EXERCISES. SKIP ANY EXERCISES THAT FEEL TOO DIFFICULT OR ARE UNINTERESTING TO YOU. YOU CAN ALWAYS COME BACK.

Section I

ORIGINS OF LOVESTYLES

Understanding the origin of your lovestyle is a key to being able to consciously change it and use it more positively; and understanding it is essential to expressing it. These first exercises are for self-discovery. You'll become familiar with your own style first, then in a later section you'll learn how to make style changes as they become necessary.

EXERCISES FOR INDIVIDUALS
(Exercises to do by yourself):

Exercise No. 1

Create a journal or notebook to record your discoveries here. Make it as simple or as creative as you like—think of it as your "wish book" or a workbook to help you create the relationship of your heart's desire. There are no extra points for making this step difficult. If you like journals, make it as much fun and as beautiful as you like. If writing is not your thing, record your discoveries on tape, or just make brief notes. You'll want to have some record, though, because we'll refer back to previous exercises as we go along. This process is designed to give you a sense of your lovestyle. The self-awareness you gain through these exercises will become a valuable tool for learning to create an effective lovestyle with your beloved.

Exercise No. 2 (Part I)

When you have the luxury of time to yourself and the energy to devote to creating your perfect relationship (this is perfect for that lonely, rainy Saturday night), create a cosy surrounding, get comfortable and think back over your childhood and your life until today. Review all the times you felt loved. Even if you had a terrible childhood, surely there were *some* times when you felt loved. Kindness shown by friends, teachers, grandparents, extended family, neighbors, etc., all count. Even scenes from books, movies and television can be utilized to imagine words, actions and events that symbolize love to you. Take your time with this: fantasies and reminiscences become richer when we stay with them for a while.

When you have a collection of scenes, words and gestures that symbolize love to you, write down the essence of receiving love.

Love is:

> being understood
> physical affection (hugging, a gentle touch)
> time spent with someone special
> sentimental gifts
> eye-to-eye contact
> a surprise party
> quiet talks
> the whole family together at dinner
> phone calls for no special reason
> a card game with silly jokes and laughter
> knowing when to leave me alone, and when to offer comfort
> an energetic game of tag, hide-and-seek or touch football.

Allow plenty of time. This is research on a very important project—your life!

Consider also what was happening to other people when you thought they were getting loved. Did you think a sibling of yours, or another child in your neighborhood, got more love than you? Why? Was there something about the other child that seemed to be more lovable? What was it? How about other relatives? Did anyone else get what you wanted? Notice what you wanted.

Avoid judging your responses. Censorship does not invite openness. There is no *wrong* answer to this exercise. It's not a test, it's an information-gathering process—research. All answers are acceptable.

Exercise No. 2 (Part II)

At another time, do the other side of the exercise—focus on times when you felt *loving*. (It's important to do this, too, because often we have different criteria for being loved and being loving.) Think about people or fictional characters who fit your picture of loving people. Sort and analyze your data and add it to your journal. We'll use it later in another exercise.

Exercise No. 3 (Part I)

This is a guided meditation. You may find it helpful to record the following directions on tape and play them back for yourself. You can then experience the exercise with no distraction. Having a friend read them works well, too.

Sit quietly and comfortably, close your eyes and call up a picture of your parents (or whoever raised you). Imagine them standing side by side. Stack a pile of blocks in front of each one.

Label each block in front of your mother with one of her lovestyle attributes. For example, in front of Mother, the pile of blocks may include:

> touches easily
> smiles a lot
> nags unsuccessfully
> cooks special foods to show love
> waits up late
> helps with homework
> always there for sports and school plays; supportive.

Father's, on the other hand, may include:

> rough, backslapping sense of humor
> teases and jokes
> holds high expectations
> keeps his promises
> refuses to praise; brags about you to others instead
> rewards with money
> good provider
> honest.

Consider how your parents showed affection to each other and other relatives, as well as to their children.

Once you have the blocks labeled, let your parents recede into the background, and focus now on the blocks. Sort them into two piles: (1) those qualities you like and want to keep for yourself; and (2) those qualities you do not want to carry on. Take your time, this is an important choice.

When you finish sorting, look at the pile of qualities you want to keep. Is it complete? What does it need? That is, what are the qualities neither of your parents had but that you would like to cultivate in yourself?

Create new blocks from whatever sources you can find:

> grandparents and other relatives
> people you know today
> you as you are today
> fictional characters
> public personalities, historical and current
> teachers and other role models.

Add the admirable qualities of these people to your "keeps" pile. Put the "keeps" pile in a safe place, where you can get at it whenever you need to.

Exercise No. 3 (Part II)

Now focus on the discard pile, and do something to get rid of it permanently. You may want to give it back to your parents, or burn it or put it in the trash. Bring your parents back into the foreground and thank them for their help and their attempts to love you the best they could with what they knew. If you find it too difficult to do that, express your thanks to them for giving birth to you.

Say good-bye, and come back to everyday reality by opening your eyes.

In your journal, write down your discoveries and the list of lovestyle characteristics you've decided to keep for yourself.

EXERCISES FOR NEW RELATIONSHIPS
(Exercises to do with someone new in your life):

Exercise No. 1

Begin a book, such as a scrapbook or blank book, for your relationship discoveries and history. This book will become a record of your discoveries together: put in mementos of special occasions, cards and letters you've given each other, notes about important events and memorable happenings. Share the development of this book as much as possible, although it may well be that one of you takes more interest in it than the other; in that case, review it together from time to time.

Make this a record of your journey, a place to commemorate your accomplishments, and it will become a treasure as time goes by. There's no need to make it difficult or complicated. A sentence or two, a picture, a few mementos of a celebration or a vacation, can be enough. The point is to enjoy it, and to create a resource that you can use throughout your years together.

Exercise No. 2

This next exercise is simple to do, but a bit complicated to explain. Sit together facing each other. We are going to do a bit of role-playing, or improvisation. Each of you takes the role of your parent of the same sex. That is, if you're a man, pretend to be your father; if a woman, your mother.

We're all different and have different backgrounds. If you have some trouble with this (if, for example, your mother died when you were born and you never knew her), then be whoever took that role in your life—grandmother, aunt, foster mother, etc. Or be your parent of the opposite sex. The important thing is to take the role of someone influential to you when you were small. (If you are in a gay or lesbian relationship, the respective parents will be of the same sex when you do this.)

Now pretend that these two parents have just met. They're passing time somewhere (perhaps in a laundromat), and while they sit, they discuss their children (you). The discussion can be about the current (adult) you or the historical (child) you. The important thing is to think about the topics the way your mother or father would.

Take one minute to set your scene (the laundromat, a park bench, etc.). Then introduce yourselves to each other (as strangers who meet) and begin to talk.

Work the following topics into the conversation:

How do the kids get into trouble?

How are the kids successful (what do they do right?)

What are you, as parents, glad you taught your kids?

What do you *wish* you had taught them?

Comment on the kids' relationship history. What do you, as parents, think about it?

Please do the above before going on.

After you've finished, sit a minute and become aware of all the "stuff" you have in your mind about what your parents would think about you and what you're doing. My point is, whether you like it or not, whether you agree with it or not, that running commentary is there with you *always*. Whenever you're not thinking carefully about what you're doing, whenever you go on "automatic," it's liable to take over. That's how you wind up doing things you can't believe you're doing, saying things you don't believe, etc.

Your beliefs and prejudices about love and relationships are shaped to a large extent by this sort of internal dialogue. The good news is that you are not helpless in the face of this. You're able to pick and choose from your past experiences and reject those options you don't want to keep. Also, you can find other ways of expression, new ideas, and adopt those in place of the old undesirable ones.

After the exercise, discuss your reactions, discoveries and the changes you'd like to make. Also, consider the similarities and differences in your parents' viewpoints, and discuss where the historical aspects of your style will work well together and where they may lead to difficulties. For example, if one of you comes from a family which uses sarcasm as a form of humor, in the style of comedian Joan Rivers, and the other's family values gentleness and consideration, you may need to have a serious discussion of those differences to avoid constant mutual hurt feelings and arguments.

If this exercise works well for you, and you feel you gained insight from it, you may want to do it again, being your parent of the *opposite* sex. Or, you can think of different topics for the "parents" to discuss. The exercise is a beginning, a suggestion. Use it as a tool for self-knowledge. It can be very helpful, if you're "stuck" in a struggle over something, to have your "parents" discuss the issue. Very interesting insights emerge when you understand the underlying, subconscious pressures that are interfering with your problem-solving ability.

Remember, what is said here is only your *impression* of your parent's opinion. Your true parent might surprise you with a totally different response. And your true parent may have changed and grown considerably from the parent you adapted to as a small child. The purpose of this exercise is to clarify the subtle dialogue in *your mind*, not discover who your parents are or what they really think.

When you finish, record your most significant insights in your "memory book."

Exercise No. 3

Sit together and do a "dialogue" exercise: Person A says, "I feel loved when . . ." (Complete the sentence.) Person B responds only with "Thank you." Then B says, "I feel loved when . . ." (Complete the sentence.) A responds with "Thank you." Continue to alternate this sentence/response process, finishing the sentences differently each time.

Do this for at least five minutes, more if possible, to give yourself a chance to get into the process.

Then share your reactions.

> Were you surprised by anything you said?
> How about what your partner said? Anything surprising there?
> Did you notice that what your partner said gave you some new ideas?
> Did any themes or recurring types of lovestyle expression emerge?
> What did you notice about yourself?
> About your partner?

Remember, this is not about the right or wrong way to express love—it's about *different* ways of expressing love.

When you're through, record significant insights and reactions in your book.

Exercise No. 4

Because we put such emotional value on our holidays and "special" days (birthdays, anniversaries, etc.), we can gain insight into lovestyles by exploring celebrational and ritual styles. It can be very enlightening and useful to spend time discussing the ways our families celebrated or commemorated holidays. Done *before* the approach of a special occasion, this exercise can save a lot of confusion and grief.

Here's how to discover your holiday styles:

First, choose a particular holiday or "special" day as your topic. Review it initially from your history, your childhood.

When this occasion drew near, did you anticipate it happily or did you worry about it? Or were your feelings mixed?

Was it very clear what you were "supposed" to do, or was there a feeling of confusion or creative freedom?

What aspects of this event did you enjoy?

What aspects did you dislike?

Of the aspects you liked or disliked, do you feel differently about them now that you are an adult?

When you hear the name of this holiday (Christmas, birthday, anniversary, graduation, etc.), what symbols come to mind? ("It wouldn't be Chanukah without Mother's latkes.")

Was there special clothing to wear? food to eat? Places to go?

Were people around for this event who were not around normally?

What other components of this time seem significant to you?

The point is to discuss how these celebrations were conducted and to clearly understand the differences between your backgrounds. We'll do more with this information in the section on "Synthesis." In the meantime, notice how different your families were and how they were similar. Most important is to notice how many options there are for celebrating special occasions. If just the two of you have this many options, how many more must there be in the world?

As always, record your findings in the "memory book."

Exercise No. 5

This exercise is similar to the last one. I use the prior exercise as a warmup, because it's usually easier to conceptualize style as it's expressed in concrete events. What you're going to discuss here is the expression of love, otherwise known as lovestyles.

To begin, picture a typical week in your childhood family life. What you're looking for are expressions of love. For our purposes here, we're not concerned with whether or not they *felt* loving to you, but only with whether or not they were meant to *convey* love. For example, if you have a weight problem now, your mother's insistence that you eat may not feel like a loving gesture to you; but to her, it was probably an attempt to express her love.

Was there a difference between weekdays and weekends? Did you have to wait until the right day to express or receive love?

Did your family talk? Was it OK to say "I love you," or were you supposed to show it subtly?

Was it loving to be aggressive and force yourself upon others who "needed love," or were you supposed to love people by "giving them room"?

How were illness, disappointment and sorrow handled?

What was done to express joy and happiness when you were together?

How were "good-byes" handled? Homecomings?

Was there a lot of emphasis on being together as a family?

You're not talking about the right or wrong way to love, remember, merely about different ways your families did it. The object is *understanding*. There are many more questions to ask in addition to the above. Invent some questions of your own and answer them.

EXERCISES FOR LONGTERM RELATIONSHIPS
(Exercises to do together with a longterm partner):

Exercise No. 1

Read Exercise 1 for New Relationships about starting a memory book. Set up a similar book for your relationship: you can go through your mementos and add past memories to it, or just begin it from here. Remember, make it easy and fun—there's no need to turn this into a chore.

This book is for *you*—it won't be graded or criticized. It'll be used fondly in years to come. Allow the whole family to participate if you like; or have two books: one for the family and one private, just for the two of you. Or you can make just one book for the two of you.

When I give you an instruction to add the results of an exercise to this book, remember it's for your future reference: you don't need to go into great detail—just enough information to help you remember what you've discovered is sufficient.

Exercise No. 2

Get out the photo albums, or other mementos of your time together, get comfortable and begin a discussion. As you review your time with each other, think back to your own parents.

How does your relationship compare? What are the similarities? The differences?

Do you like the similarities and differences?

Would you like to add anything that your parents did?

Would you like to stop emulating them in any way?

Remember, the answers to these questions will be different for each of you. Keep your focus on the comparison of your relationship and your respective parents' relationships. We'll explore other changes later. Select certain pictures or mementos to put in your memory book, or write a few sentences describing what your discoveries are.

Exercise No. 3

Consider all the other relationships (friends, relatives) you have knowledge about, and compare their lovestyles to yours.

Have any of these other options given you ideas about love and its expression?

Have you tried to imitate them?

How did it work?

Is there anything you've seen others do that you'd like to add to your relationship?

Is there anything you've seen in others that you're afraid might happen in your relationship?

The people around us express their love in tremendously varied ways, and those expressions, when we encounter them, often influence us, consciously and unconsciously.

This exercise will help you to be aware of these influences, so that what you absorb into your own life is consciously chosen. Summarize your observations and conclusions in your book.

Exercise No. 4

Sit together and have a dialogue: Partner A says, "I feel loved by you when . . ." (Complete the sentence.) Partner B says, "Thank you." Then Partner B says, "I feel loved by you when . . ." (Complete the sentence.) Partner A says, "Thank you." Repeat these exchanges alternately for about ten or fifteen minutes. The "thank you" responses are to prevent you from praising, criticizing, blaming, making excuses or otherwise commenting, positively or negatively, on your partner's statement.

Say your sentence and complete it as quickly as you can, back and forth, and after a few minutes you'll find that your ideas flow smoothly. If you get stuck, just say "pass" and go on to the next round.

After doing this, discuss what you've learned:

Were there any surprises?

Did you get any good ideas from your partner's statements?

How did you feel, hearing how your partner felt loved?

How did you feel, sharing how you felt loved?

The above questions are not essential. In your own words, discuss what you learned from the exchange. Use my sample questions just to get started. As usual, condense and include in your book.

Exercise No. 5

Now, do the same exercise as (4), but use the sentence, "I know I love you when . . ." Both partners take turns completing the sentence, and both make the "thank you" response.

Again discuss the results; this time, pay attention to the *differences* between when you feel loving and when you feel loved. Don't be surprised that there are differences. Most people have different ways of giving than of receiving. In fact, when you observe the differences, you may want to make some changes, to learn to give and receive in various ways.

SECTION II

YOUR INDIVIDUAL, UNIQUE LOVESTYLE

These exercises are designed to help you separate your own personal lovestyle from the styles of your parents and others who influenced you. They'll help you understand what you've been doing until now. Before you make changes, it's wise to fully understand the current process.

EXERCISES FOR INDIVIDUALS

Exercise No. 1

In your journal, write a letter to your past, your childhood, thanking it for its lessons, expressing any anger, pain, appreciation, regret, etc., you feel as a result of your experience there. Add some gratitude to yourself as a child for surviving as well as you have. Perhaps you'd like to mention some things you're particularly glad you received, and also some things you wish to leave behind or change.

Close the letter by saying good-bye to the past and hello to your life as it is today. In this way, you can symbolically "own" your current life and give yourself "permission" to be totally in charge of what happens now, regardless of how things happened then.

If there's too much inner turmoil for you to do this, then first write a "rough draft," in which you outline all the turbulence, all the pros and cons, anger and resentment, confusion and fear. After you've done that, refine it down to a letter which will let you achieve some "closure." Do as many sessions of writing as you need to feel complete.

It's important to know that you can still work on events and incidents in your past without invalidating this letter. This is a symbolic way of taking responsibility for making your life and relationships what you want them to be from now on. If writing a letter is too difficult or uncomfortable for you, you can talk into a tape recorder.

As with all these exercises, *Please don't make it too difficult for yourself!* If something comes up that feels overwhelming to you, get some help from a friend or counselor.

Exercise No. 2

Have another reverie: this time, go back into your past to see how you were unique.

What made you feel different from all the other people in your family? School? Friends?

When did the differences feel good?

When did the differences feel bad?

How did you know you were special?

Can you remember anyone talking about how different you were?

Did anyone ever urge you to "be like your brother (sister, cousin, neighbor's child, etc.)"? How were you being different when they said that?

After you've explored these unique aspects of yourself for a while, make some notes in your journal about how you learned you were special when you were a child, both the positive and negative ways. If you like, you can make two separate lists.

Exercise No. 3

Give yourself some time between the last exercise and this one. (You may want to read the following instructions into your tape recorder and play them back.) Get comfortable, sit back and relax and take a "magical journey" through your life from your childhood up to now.

Imagine your life as a game board. On it, there's a winding pathway with brightly colored cartoons along the way symbolizing the events that feel significant to you. In the center of the board are two piles of cards: one is marked "lessons" and the other is marked "gifts." Choose a gamepiece to represent you, and travel the board. Each time you arrive at an event, draw a card marked "lesson," read it and notice what it says. Once you've understood the lesson, draw a "gift" card and read it.

Let your imagination run free, and don't censor what the cards tell you. If a card is blank, just put it aside and draw another. Do this until you reach the point on the board that represents your life now, then open your eyes.

Take a moment to review the game, then record significant parts of it in your book. Once you've done that, review the "game" again, and this time watch yourself change as you pass along the journey.

When you were a child, would you have believed you'd turn out as you have?

Would the child you were recognize the adult you are now?

What would be the same? What would be different?

Do you think the same way about play as you did?

How has your definition of friends changed?

Has your idea of what's fun or pleasurable changed?

Have you forgotten or "lost" anything you'd like to reclaim for yourself?

How have you improved yourself?

Take some time to consider the changes you've created in yourself throughout the magical journey of your life, and when you've thought it over, make notes in your journal. *Please give yourself plenty of credit for making lots of powerful changes in yourself.* Also note changes you'd still like to make.

Exercise No. 4

In your journal, write a description of your "perfect relationship." One way to do this is to make a series of lists or paragraphs about it, listing the necessary characteristics, such as:

Good communication: when we make a joint decision, there's no confusion.

Playing sports together: tennis, backpacking, bicycling. Lots of quiet time together.

etc.

If you use the "list method," be specific and accurate enough to have a clear picture of the relationship when you're done.

The other method, which I prefer, is to write a story about a perfect week together. Be as specific as possible and involve all your senses. What do the scenes in your story look like? Sound like (music, conversation, etc.)? Feel like (peaceful, exhilarating, etc.)? Taste the foods you'd eat together; smell the outdoor air, the ocean breeze, the fireplace.

Perhaps you can begin with a regular working Monday:

What's the first thing you'd do in the morning? Would you get up and jog together? Make love? Maybe you'd cuddle till the last minute and then rush off to work. Or perhaps you prefer lots of "space" when you get up.

Would you go off to work together? To your joint business? To separate jobs? Would one of you (or both) stay home with the children? The only limits here are the ones you set yourself.

After work, would you go out to dinner? Eat at home? Take classes? See friends? Relax alone together?

Get the idea? Go through a whole week and weekend like that, and perhaps a vacation or a holiday. Remember, this fantasy is not about what you *think* you could have or what you think you deserve. It's about *the perfect relationship.* You may surprise yourself when you get into this exercise.

Go back to the results of the other exercises and use that information to help do this one. How do you know when you're being loved? That is an important aspect of the perfect relationship. So is knowing when you're loving. Allow yourself plenty of chances to be loved and to be loving.

Take some time with this, ponder it, revise it frequently as you learn. This fantasy will help you recognize when your real relationships are working for you.

Be careful not to get so idealistic that you come up with a lifestyle you wouldn't find comfortable. Stick with what you want, not what you think you *should* want. Consider practical, economic, educational, social and cultural factors, as well as romance and sexuality. Live with this exercise a while before going on to the next. It deserves time and careful thought, because it's a key to achieving contentment and recognizing success.

Exercise No. 5

Now, again in your journal, consider the perfect mate. This will naturally be someone who would be comfortable in the lifestyle described in your perfect relationship. Do you see how considering the relationship before considering the person makes sense? If you've put certain shared hobbies and interests into your ideal relationship, then someone who is already interested in these activities would be a good person to find. If you're looking for a mate, then look among people who fit your desired lifestyle. Such people will probably fit *you* better, too.

If you already have a mate who is interested in those shared things, recognize the importance of that. If your mate is not interested, consider other ways you can bring those activities into your life—playing tennis with friends, for example.

It's OK to consider characteristics such as looks and dress style when outlining your perfect mate, but remember that living with a person on a lifetime basis involves a lot more than just how he or she looks. It's also OK to be vague about some of these qualities. You may not have a preference about blonde or brown hair, but you may want a particular body style. Or you may not care too much about looks, but education may be very important. Just be sure you get specific about the things that count for you.

Some of you may come up with a perfect relationship that calls for more than one ideal mate. OK. Do this exercise for however many mates you want. If you want them each to be different, describe how. The important thing is that you know what you want when you're done.

For those of you with mates already chosen, consider how your partner is already perfect for you. Most of us chose well enough; we just haven't figured out how to use what we've got. If you're already paired up, this exercise will give you a starting place to begin to bring your ideal and your real relationships into alignment.

Sort through people, friends, relatives, public figures, former loves, etc., for the qualities you find desirable in your mate. Pick and choose until you come up with a description that works for you.

Live with the idea a while, then revise it if necessary. Discuss it with trusted friends, sharing whichever parts of it you like, and get their ideas. It's worth spending some time on this, for if you're single, it'll greatly influence how you look at possible candidates from now on. For one thing, it'll make it necessary to look a bit deeper than just appearance before deciding who's appropriate for you. For another, it'll influence where and how you look.

This description of your ideal mate is not going to be used in a pass/fail sense. It's possible that your true mate will vary widely from this description. What you have here is a starting place, to give you some idea of criteria, and to make it obvious to you when you're staying with someone who will never satisfy you only because you're afraid to move on.

When you have a description that suits you for now (you can always revise it as you learn), pause a moment and consider what you've learned from doing this.

Are you surprised?

Is what would work for you different from what you thought you wanted?

What is the difference?

Has this helped you clear up confusion about the difference between what you "should" want and what would really satisfy you?

Add these conclusions to your journal, and give yourself

some time to absorb and process this material before going on to the next section.

EXERCISES FOR NEW RELATIONSHIPS

Exercise No. 1

Sit quietly for a moment and imagine that you're leaving your childhood today. This is a ceremonial occasion, and you're packing your bag. Consider the aspects of childhood, both tangible (material) and intangible (qualities of life, feelings, etc.).

Then discuss the following questions:

What would you take?

What would you like to leave behind?

Are there any surprises?

Recap this discussion for your relationship book.

Exercise No. 2

Now consider your previous relationship experience.

How much childhood baggage did you take with you into your past relationship?

How much of it was helpful?

How much was a hindrance?

What about your previous partners' baggage?

What past hassles would you like to avoid in this relationship?

What past peaks would you like to recreate?

Recap for your book.

Exercise No. 3

Consider what makes you different from anyone you know, and share these special qualities of yours with your partner. Then tell your partner what you think is unique about him/her. If you like, confess something that you feel silly or "weird" about in the way you express or receive love. Checking your notes from the "I feel loved/loving when . . ." exercise can be helpful here.

It's possible to really get into this exercise, for what you're doing here is describing aspects of your own, unique lovestyle—and describing how your partner's lovestyle looks to you, with emphasis on its uniqueness.

After you've discussed this for a while, make a page in the book for the lovestyle of each of you. Take a whole page or more, and title it with your name. Make it as expressive, funny, dramatic or appropriate to your style as possible.

Being silly about this, making a game of it or drawing pictures may help you communicate about your unique styles more effectively. Perhaps you may want to do "impersonations" of each other, to dramatize your observations. If so, keep this as light as you can—and watch out for hurt feelings or misunderstandings. If confusion occurs, stop and clear it up before you continue. All this can be done in an atmosphere of love and learning.

Exercise No. 4

The purpose of this next exercise is to help you achieve a

sense of detachment, so you can discover your sense of purpose. If you're uncomfortable with the metaphor of death, you can change it accordingly, or skip the exercise entirely.

I've noticed that doing this exercise in classes and workshops brings up strong feelings, so do it gently and take ample time.

Imagine your own memorial service, or a time after your death when your family and friends, all the people you loved and who loved you, are gathered together, remembering you.

How would you like them to remember you?

What would you want them to say about you?

What would you want them to miss, now that you've gone?

What impression would you like to leave on the larger public—your neighborhood, town, country, the world, etc.?

How would that differ from the impression left with your family and friends?

This is an opportunity to imagine your life, past, present and future, in its entirety, and what effect you would like to have had on people. Looking at this fantasy of your life as a whole will give you the benefit of a detached point of view. As a result, you'll have an idea of what qualities of life are truly important to you, especially concerning love.

After taking sufficient time to view your own life, share your experiences with your partner, including what was difficult for you, what you learned, and what meaning you see in it all.

In our day-to-day preoccupation with the details of living,

we can lose sight of the larger picture. This kind of fantasy, thoughtfully done, can give you a sense of the impact your life can have on the people you care about.

As always, record the results in your book.

EXERCISES FOR LONGTERM RELATIONSHIPS

Exercise No. 1

Consider what makes you different from anyone you know, and share these special qualities of yours with your partner. Then tell your partner what you think is unique about him/her. If you like, confess something that you feel silly or "weird" about in the way you express or receive love. Checking your notes from the "I feel loved/loving when . . ." exercise can be helpful here.

It's possible to really get into this exercise, for what you're doing here is describing aspects of your own, unique lovestyle—and describing how your partner's lovestyle looks to you, with emphasis on the uniqueness.

After you've discussed this for a while, make a page in the book for the lovestyle of each of you. Take a whole page or more, and title it with your name. Make it as expressive, funny, dramatic or appropriate to your style as possible.

Also record any changes you've noticed in your lovestyle or your partner's in the time you've been together. You have the advantage of having known each other intimately for a while—this makes you excellent resources for each other.

Being silly about this, making a game of it or drawing pictures may help you communicate about your unique styles more effectively. Perhaps you may want to do "impersona-tions" of each other, to dramatize your observations. If so, keep this as light as you can—and watch out for hurt feel-ings or misunderstandings.

If confusion occurs, stop and clear it up before you con-tinue. All this can be done in an atmosphere of love and learning.

Exercise No. 2

The purpose of this next exercise is to help you achieve a sense of detachment, so you can discover your sense of pur-pose. If you're uncomfortable with the metaphor of death, you can change it accordingly, or skip the exercise entirely.

This is likely to bring up some strong feelings, at least it has when I've done it, so do it gently and take ample time.

Imagine your own memorial service, or a time after your death when your family and friends, all the people you loved and who loved you, are gathered together, remem-bering you.

How would you like them to remember you?

What would you want them to say about you?

What would you want them to miss, now that you've gone?

What impression would you like to leave on the larger public—your neighborhood, town, country, the world, etc.?

How would that differ from the impression left with your family and friends?

This is an opportunity to imagine your life, past, present and future, in its entirety, and what effect you would like to have had on people. Looking at this fantasy of your life as a whole will give you the benefit of a detached point of view. As a result, you'll have an idea of what qualities of life are truly important to you, especially concerning love.

After taking sufficient time to view your own life, share your experiences with your partner, including what was difficult for you, what you learned, and what meaning you see in it all.

In our day-to-day preoccupation with the details of living, we can lose sight of the larger picture. This kind of fantasy, thoughtfully done, can give you a sense of the impact your life can have on the people you care about.

As always, record the results in your book.

Exercise No. 3

Richard and I enjoy doing the following ceremony on New Year's Eve, and on our anniversary. You may want to make it an ongoing part of your relationship, too.

Get some paper and pencils. If you have a fireplace, get two small paper bags—if not, a large ashtray and some matches. (In warm weather, we sometimes use our charcoal grill outside.)

You'll also need a monthly or daily calendar that stays in one place (on a wall or desk). The calendar must include a date one year from today. If it's December 31, 1987, you need a calendar that includes December 31, 1988.

Each of you is going to write two lists. The first list is what you'd like to eliminate from your relationship—hassles, difficulties, deprivations, etc.

The second list is what you'd like to bring into or create in your relationship to replace what you're releasing or to add to what you already have.

Make two separate lists, on separate pieces of paper. Think of them as what you wish to let go of (the "old") and what you wish to bring in (the "new").

Take your time, and when you're done, share the contents of the lists. Go gently on the "elimination list"—remember, you're eliminating your own hassles. Take responsibility and phrase them in terms of yourself ("I messages"), rather than your partner ("you messages"). For example: "I want to eliminate hassles about the kitchen being dirty," instead of, "I want you to stop messing up the kitchen."

Maintain an atmosphere of sharing, a lightness; this is not a problem-solving session. This exercise works more on the subconscious and intuitive levels than the rational, thinking level.

Once you've written and shared your lists, crumple up the "elimination" list. If you have a fire in a fireplace, get your paper bag, put the list in it, blow in some air, twist the top tight and toss it in the fire. It will "pouf" into flame and be consumed. As it does this, say out loud, "I release this energy into the universe to be transformed into something more useful." If you have no fire or fireplace, simply light your list with a match or from a candle and place it in the big ashtray or the barbeque. Use the same phrase as above, said aloud as the list burns.

Do this as ceremoniously as you like. If you like tradition and ritual, have music, candles, incense, etc. Make your lists as simple or as fancy and artistic as you wish. If you're religious, include a reference to your God. For example, you can turn your "release" list over to Jesus, or to the Gohanzin, and ask for your "creations" from the same source.

Then, take your "creation" lists and tape them on the calendar page one year from today's date. There's nothing more to do for one year, until that day rolls around.

On that day, take out your lists, and you'll be surprised at how much of what you wanted to create you've accomplished. Richard and I find this a delightful, encouraging process to do twice a year. We include lots of friends in the New Year's Eve ceremony but keep our wedding anniversary ceremony private.

If you like, you can just make a note on your calendar, and keep your lists in your book instead. Then you can ceremoniously take out the book and look at the lists on the appointed date.

Exercise No. 4

Together, make a list of all the social "rules" ("It's not nice to . . .") that keep you from doing things you'd really like to do. For example, if you didn't have to face your family and friends, would you quit your job and sail around the world? Or would you become a stripper? A movie star? A doctor or lawyer? A sheik with a harem?

Take some time to fantasize together about all the things you'd do if it was really OK to do them. Remember, this is only fantasy. You don't actually have to act on them.

When you've made your lists, check it out to see if there's a part of you that's not being expressed and look for a "safe" way to express it. Your partner, who is likely to have a different set of taboos than you, may be able to help you think of ways to do what you want that don't have unpleasant consequences for you.

For example, if your private dream is to be an actor, perhaps there's an emotive, dramatic side of you that you're not expressing. There's an obvious solution: getting involved in little theatre locally, or working with a local high school to help them put on plays. (They always need dedicated volunteers.) There's also the less obvious solution of taking a more vocal role in your church, your job, or joining Toastmasters. There are many "ordinary" aspects of life that require dramatic flair and talent.

In doing this exploration together, you'll probably gain more insight into yourself and your partner, and vice versa. Quite often, we tend to think that our uniqueness is "wrong" or "bad" when it's really quite possible to express it positively. That expression can enrich your life when it's done in a way that works for you.

Together, negotiate and draw up a contract for more self-expression. In the contract, decide what you want to achieve. Keep it as simple as possible, for now. You can always add to it later. Determine what help and support you can give each other in achieving these goals, and also where else you might be able to find support and/or information.

The more possible you make these goals, the more enthusiastic you'll be, and the more chance you have of success! When you feel you have a workable contract, write it in your book and sign it. Set up some dates for the first steps to be accomplished. Good luck!

SECTION III

CHANGES: REDESIGNING YOUR LOVESTYLE

What happens if you discover in Sections I and II that your lovestyle, as you've been practicing it, is not very compatible with who *you* are? Or that most of it is, but there are one or two areas in which you feel stifled and unexpressed?

Simple. You can change your lovestyle! Mostly, it just takes thought and practice to change your mode of expression. I'm not talking about changing your feelings and reactions, just your method of communicating them and/or acting upon them. With some experimentation and thought, you can figure out what the necessary changes are and practice new patterns until you're comfortable with them.

Any change is uncomfortable at first, so you must be prepared to deal with the newness, but lots of people have done it before you, and so can you. It's no harder than learning a new job, or how to react to a new friend, or starting school or a career. If you're gentle with yourself (and each other), you can make the changes you desire painlessly.

One thing I want to caution you about: If it works, don't fix it. Please don't think that you *must* make changes in your lovestyle just because you're reading this.

EXERCISES FOR INDIVIDUALS

Exercise No. 1

This is where you'll really use your journal. Go back and

review all the prior exercises. What you're looking for are differences between what actually *works* for you and what you've been doing. By way of illustration, here's a letter I received from a client I worked with a year ago:

> Dear Tina,
>
> I spent time with myself & thinking about *what makes me happy*. The roller-coaster ride finally ended, no more searching for "exciting" men. A few months later I met T_____, a man I would have considered too tame for me.
>
> I am now very content with the new lifestyle I chose *for me*.
>
> T_____ and I are married and we have a three-week-old daughter. My husband is nurturing, dependable, open-minded and able to communicate honestly, from the heart.
>
> Thank you for your help and your friendship.

The only help I gave this woman was to help her focus on what she *really needed* to be happy and how different that was from what she *thought* she needed. She did all the rest herself.

The object of your journal review is to do what she did. Go back to the early exercises, look at what actually feels like love to you. Then check out how you've managed your relationships to date and the kind of people you've picked to be with. In your journal, make a list of your needs, and next to each need put the characteristic your partner would have to have to allow him/her to satisfy that need. For example:

MY NEED	QUALITY IN LOVER
affection	comfortable with touching, hugging, holding
verbal communication	likes to talk

And so on. When you have your list done, compare it with your description of the "perfect lover" and see if it's similar. There's a good chance it will be, because of the process we used to define your perfect lover. If not, evaluate the differences and see what you want to adjust, add or subtract in your description of the perfect lover. Take your time; this is an important step.

Also, remember that you need certain things to feel *loving.* Be sure and include these on your list. Your mate needs to be comfortable receiving what you like to give, as well as giving what you like to receive.

Because we're not talking personally, this may sound very rigid and humorless. The truth is, these are simply guidelines to give you an idea of what you're looking for, and to separate what you actually *want* from what you think you *should have.* Of course, you don't just hand this list to a potential mate and say, "Here. You must meet these requirements."

Scott, a client who found his ideal mate (they've been together a year now), told me he cleaned out a closet when they moved in together, and he found his list then, more than a year after he first drew it up. He was amazed when he looked at it and found that his lover was *exactly what he wanted,* according to his list.

The real power in this exercise is self-awareness. Once you've thought these things out and know what your real needs are, that awareness becomes part of your thought process and guides you. Without a struggle, you'll be noticing different things about people, and will automatically give those with the proper qualities for you more of a chance to get to know you.

For those of you already in a relationship, the process is slightly different. Your awareness will help you begin to reshape the relationship you already have, and to get out of the trap of denying yourself activities and interests because your partner doesn't share your enthusiasm.

Many of your needs can be met by people who are not romantic interests in your life. Sports, theatre, lively discussions, etc., don't require romantic attachment. Your new awareness of your needs will encourage you to broaden your base of activities and thereby remove some of the hidden pressures in your relationship.

So, after you've made your list, go on to the next exercise.

Exercise No. 2

Here's another fantasy journey: (You may prefer to tape the following directions, and then play them back to yourself, or have a friend read them to you.) Close your eyes, relax, let your body get comfortable. Imagine a long, winding road. Take enough time to picture the scene. What is your road made of? Is it paved? What kind of land does your road run through? Countryside? Desert? City? Is there greenery along the road?

When you're clear about the scene, begin to travel along the road. As you travel, you'll encounter your former relationships, one at a time. See each one walking toward you on the journey and spend a few minutes with each one. Ask the following questions: What did I learn from you? What was it about you I enjoyed? What was it about you I couldn't handle or didn't like? How well do you match my lovestyle? Take your time with each person. As you finish with each one, thank him/her and say goodbye before traveling on to the next.

As you go back in time, you may be surprised to find your parent of the opposite sex on the road. Don't worry about it, just ask your questions. This parent is often the model for most of our later relationships, so it's important that he/she be there.

When you've traveled your entire road, allow yourself to come back to the present, bringing the answers with you.

Immediately, before the picture becomes vague, write your experience in your journal.

After you've written your discoveries down, look for trends; for example: "Every time I find someone who's enough fun, she has no sense of commitment." Or, "Men who are exciting at first turn out to be stressful in the long run." Or, "I love spending every minute together for a while, but then I begin to feel trapped." Summarize this in your book, with emphasis on what you've learned about getting what you really need instead of what you think you should have.

Allow this to settle in for a while before going on to the next exercise.

Exercise No. 3

Based on the information gathered in the last exercise, list the new criteria you've set up in order to achieve a better match if you're single, or to make your current relationship more satisfying, if you're coupled.

Consider your list a moment, then make a list of ways to meet people who'll meet your needs. For example, if you want someone emotionally expressive, perhaps amateur theatre groups, volunteer organizations that work with the physically or emotionally challenged, or other activity groups that attract a "feeling" type of person would be a good place for you to spend your time. You could learn something, contribute to society and find a partner, all at the same time.

If sports or dancing are an important part of your life (or you'd like them to be), then sports clubs, dance studios, etc., would be places to go.

To find someone who thinks friends are important, who likes the "family" feeling of lots of time spent with good friends, get yourself invited to your friends' parties. If you have few friends of your own, then that's a place to start, for as you make friends, you increase your chances of meeting a person who thinks the way you do about friendship.

Got the idea? The point is to put yourself in a location that maximizes your chances of meeting "Mr./Ms. Right," or increases the possibility of making friends who enhance your current relationship.

I have two dear friends who met in a singles bar and who have been happily married now for ten years. However, they are the *only* two people I know who successfully met in a bar and created a satisfying longterm relationship. It is possible, but is it likely that you'll meet your heart's desire in a bar? Consider the percentages.

There are endless activities, interests, hobbies, volunteer jobs, classes, etc., in which you'll automatically be placed in close proximity to others who are interested in the same things. Meeting people in this way eliminates the stress of the "cold" approach to a stranger, and automatically takes care of the preliminary screening for you. If you don't drink, a bar's not a good place to meet someone who is like-minded (nondrinkers do go to bars to dance or be social, but the odds aren't very good there).

Write your conclusions in your book. You're beginning to form a plan of action. Allow for "percolation" time before going on.

Exercise No. 4

When clients come to me looking for a partner or frustrated by their current relationship, the first thing I always tell them is to take a good look at themselves and their lives. Look around your home. Whether or not it's luxurious is not the important thing. Look around to see what it says about you.

If you're a conversationalist, does your home invite guests to be comfortable and talk? Is there a space that makes conversation easy and natural? If all your chairs are far apart, how can you comfortably encourage conversation with your new friends?

What does your home say about *you?* Does it look as if you

live there, or does it feel anonymous? Will a visitor to your home learn good things about you from its atmosphere? Will he/she be curious to learn more?

And what about your life? What do you have to offer? Do you have a life someone else will think is worth sharing? Do some of your leisure activities allow company to join you? Looking at your lifestyle, would someone be moved to say, "That looks like fun! I'd like to get in on that!" If you've been looking for someone for a long time without results, or if you have a relationship but few friends, you've probably been focusing on the "other person" and not on yourself. All your energy has been going into what you want your *partner* to be and do, and not on what *you* want to be and do.

Your first priority is to get your own life together. Start with your body and your health. You don't have to dress in the latest fashion, but learn to be well-groomed, clean and attractive.

Then, focus on your home. Make it a place you'd be proud to invite people to, and keep it that way. The day you meet a new friend, or even Mr./Ms. Right, you don't want to miss out because your home is too embarrassing to invite him/her over for coffee. Have things in your home you're eager to show people, so you can be enthusiastic about your invitation.

Definitely don't make the bedroom the only place of interest. It could be the pièce de résistance; don't set it up to be just a fast snack. Also, if you're only interested in being friends with this new person, a spectacular bedroom in an otherwise dull home could be very misleading.

Set up a cosy place in your living room for conversation and relaxation; then, if you like, burn a candle or some incense there to concentrate your energy and focus your thoughts on your entire life and what you want.

Your activities, work, relaxation, should all come under the same scrutiny in turn. By this time, you'll be feeling so good about yourself and your life, the anxiety about finding a partner will fade. Then, voilà! The magic happens. Why? Because you're relaxed and happy, and that's the most fascinating and attractive you can be. You'll have a choice of potential partners and friends.

To describe the effect more clearly, I like to use this metaphor of "squirrel hunting": There are two ways to catch squirrels: (1) You can run all over and try to grab them or pounce on them, but you'll only scare them away, and they'll run faster than you every time. In the end you'll be very frustrated and exhausted, with no squirrels.

Or (2) you can go to where they are, offer them something attractive like walnuts, and wait quietly, just enjoying the day and the place. It'll take a while, but when they see you're very comfortable, relaxed and quiet, they'll begin to get curious, and soon they'll begin to "check you out."

Stay relaxed, let them get to know you're no threat and that you have goodies, and before long they'll be all over you, eating out of your hand. Then you'll have your choice of several squirrels. Success is guaranteed, if you have a little patience.

It really isn't much different finding friends or a partner. More depends on how you feel about *you* and your own life, being satisfied with yourself, than on how rich or handsome you are. Physical looks and outer attributes fade in importance very quickly—your personality and self-esteem are what others really value. Good grooming is important, however, because it's an outward expression of your feelings about yourself. Building up your opinion of yourself will enhance your current relationship, your friendships and/or any new relationships.

Allow some time to do this review—you deserve the attention from yourself. Write your observations in your book and note the changes you'd like to make.

Exercise No. 5

Now, the plan of "attack": In this exercise, you'll follow the Four Steps to Success, which are necessary to reach any goal. They are:

(1) Choose the goal.

(2) Break it down into small, nonintimidating steps.

(3) Do something. (If you can't get yourself to do it, you haven't made the steps small or easy enough—go back to step 2.)

(4) Celebrate what you've done (yes, every little step).

From the activities in the last two exercises, choose one to begin with. For example, suppose you're interested in physical activity and music and choose a folk-dancing class. Break the goal down into manageable steps: (1) Call around to find out what classes are available; (2) choose a class to attend; (3) enroll in the class; (4) go to the first class meeting; (5) evaluate the class as to whether it's a good one for your purposes.

Those steps may seem simplistic, but that's the idea. *Make it as easy as possible to do each step.* That way you won't be discouraged by "I can't" before you start.

Breaking your goal down into the smallest possible steps makes it easier to accomplish the next phase: *Do something.* Many of us know how to set goals, but not how to achieve them, so we've "proved" to ourselves over and over that we're failures. That's not true at all. The failure lies in not having completed the rest of the Four Steps to Success.

You've just made the third step to your goal as simple as possible, so there are no reasons not to take it. Go ahead, and focus on the third step only: *Do something.*

After you've taken the third step, *celebrate.* Recognition of what you've accomplished is important. You can also celebrate each step you take toward your goal as you take it. This way you won't run out of energy before you achieve success, and you'll keep encouraging yourself as you proceed.

Your celebration can be just looking into your mirror and saying, "Congratulations, you've just made the first (second, third) step toward finding your mate (or achieving satisfaction in your relationship)." Or your celebration can be more elaborate, such as toasting your accomplishment with a friend or two. It can even be a major party. The important thing is that you do *something* to make sure you notice you've had some success, however small. It is this celebration that will give you the courage and confidence to go on all the way in achieving your goal.

Write this plan down in your book, including how you intend to celebrate. As you achieve your goal, go back to the

Four Steps and choose a new goal; then follow the steps through again. Repeat this until you've met your "perfect match," or filled your life to a satisfactory extent.

EXERCISES FOR NEW RELATIONSHIPS

Exercise No. 1

Do this exercise separately at first, then share your results. Individually, review Section I, "New Relationships," Exercise No. 3: "I feel loved/loving when . . ." Make a list of each way you feel loved and loving (or use the list you made when you originally did that exercise). Opposite each item, comment on what you *actually have done* in the past to receive and show love, and how well it worked for you.

Because we often have confusing information about what's OK in a relationship, you're likely to find some differences between what actually feels like love to you, and what you've actually been doing. Evaluate your responses individually, then discuss your conclusions together.

Exercise No. 2

Using your lists and discussion from the previous exercise, make some decisions about what you'd like to change about yourself in order to bring what you've been doing closer to what would really be effective for both of you.

If you have some fears left over from past relationships, this is a good time to share them. For example, if you were in love with an alcoholic, or had an alcoholic parent, you can share your fears and anger about what happened in that relationship, and let your partner know where your "touchy" areas are.

Discover how you can help each other avoid the "Disaster Equation" (see Part I, Chapter 4) and make an agreement to let each other know when your expressions of love are not being effective or appreciated. This is a learning process, to help you learn the art of loving each other.

Even more important, remember to let each other know when you *are* successful at feeling loved or loving. Point out all the things on your list that work well in your relationship, and give the positive side equal time.

Keep your agreements simple, and *possible*. Be careful not to get overzealous and promise things you're not likely to be able or willing to deliver. We're building a successful pattern for your relationship here, not one that will leave you feeling stressed.

If there are ways either or both of you would like to feel loved, and the other is unable or unwilling to express love in that way, then work together to find another way to be satisfied. If you'd like cards and flowers, for example, and your partner is uncomfortable with that, then perhaps you could let friends know that you'd like cards and flowers occasionally. Your partner could agree not to interfere with that, or even help you let friends know.

Remember, cooperation and mutual helpfulness are the keys here. This is not about who's right or wrong (both of you are right about yourselves), but about what will be *effective* between you. This process may take more than one try: we've all been taught far more about competing with each other than cooperating, and we've also been taught to be critical of others and consequently defensive.

This exercise, like all the others, is meant to help make your relationship flow more smoothly, not to create new problems. It's about sharing yourself, not about making demands. Remember that this new partner is not the same person(s) you had trouble with in the past and that this process can help you avoid repeating that trouble in the future.

Keep the atmosphere light and the focus on learning while you do this. It can be fun, informative and loving. If you find yourselves in a power struggle rather than a learning question, you may want to see the problem-solving section of *How to Be a Couple and Still Be Free* (Tessina and Smith, Newcastle, 1980) or get some professional help.

Write your agreements in your book.

Exercise No. 3

Imagine what will happen if you and your partner get your relationship "right." If all your dreams come true with each other, how will that be?

Discuss the following hopes and dreams:

What will your tenth year together be like? Your twentieth?

What are your financial goals together?

What kinds of friends will you have?

How will your leisure time be spent?

Make up a few questions of your own.

Now, take a moment and think about how you'll know

when you've succeeded. What milestones along the way will tell you you're headed in the right direction? If you come up with a general answer, such as, "I'll feel loved and secure," ask yourself what the outward manifestations will be when you're loved and secure. How will you know, how will your partner know? "I'll laugh a lot," or "Friends will say I'm relaxed and calm" are possibilities.

What you're doing is developing some guidelines for success and reassurance. In the near future, you'll find you've reached one of your milestones and feel greatly encouraged about what you're doing. It's a tremendous help, when facing some difficulty, to look back and see that you've accomplished some of your goals already.

Record your milestones in your journal, and mark that page for ready reference in the future.

Exercise No. 4

After doing Exercise 3, you're ready to create a celebration. Success depends upon celebration, because motivation to continue is generated by appreciation of what you've already accomplished. Once you've seen that you *can* do it, you'll be more hopeful and have more energy to take the next step.

In order to celebrate effectively, it is necessary to discover what celebration means to each of you. You can begin with a discussion of celebrations:

> celebrations that are free
> celebrations that cost money
> celebrations that are brief
> celebrations that take time.

Review Section I, "New Relationships," Exercise 4, about holidays and celebrations, to help jog your memory. Use that information to help discover the elements that make an event seem like a celebration to both of you.

When you've done that, record suggestions for future celebrations in your book. Remember to include both the on-the-spot kind and the special occasion type.

EXERCISES FOR LONGTERM RELATIONSHIPS

Exercise No. 1

In your memory book, review the previous exercises, especially Section I, "Longterm Relationships," Exercise 4: "I feel loved by you when . . ." If you haven't already made a list of the qualities of loving and being loved as they appear to you, make one for each of you and compare them.

How well have you done in the past at successfully feeling loved and letting your partner know he/she is loved? (Gently, please. The intent is to *learn*, not to criticize yourself or each other.)

Discuss your successes and your mistakes, and together help each other learn new ways of expression that will work better for you.

You'll probably find it useful to read the instructions for Section I, "New Relationships," Exercises 1 and 2. Your objective here is to avoid the "Disaster Equation" and to correct the places in your relationship where you've developed unsuccessful patterns between you.

Remember, you're not "stuck" with the patterns you have if they're not working. On the other hand, if whatever you're doing now is working, please don't fix it. No matter how good my suggestions may sound, I can't know you and your relationship as well as you do. You're the best judge of what needs to change.

Write your decisions in your book, and check them out again in a few weeks to see if they're realistic and practical for you or whether they need some adjustment.

Exercise No. 2

Discuss your ideas of how your relationship looks to others, the "public image" you project. What might your families say about you when you're not around? Your friends and neighbors? Strangers? Business associates?

How do each of you feel about this image? Is it what you want to project? Discuss any changes you'd like to make and how you could make them. Check to see if you have similar ideas about how others should see you, or if you feel differently.

Don't be surprised if other people's images of you turn out to be *better* than you want to project! In some cases, if you've been the "model couple" in your church, community or circle of friends, you may long for the freedom to relax and let others know that you *do* fight sometimes, that everything's not always perfect.

Whether you decide your image is better or worse than you'd like it to be, consider some means of letting your friends and family see the other side of things. Balance is the important quality here.

When you feel your discussion is complete, summarize it in your book.

Exercise No. 3

Discuss your picture of a perfect relationship and how you would recognize it. How will you know when you've made the changes you want to make? What signs should you look for? It's important to have clear, mutually recognizable milestones, so that you'll both know when you're successful. These "signs of success" are both encouraging and rewarding and make learning new ways of being together fun and easy.

What comments do you imagine other people you know—friends and family—will make when you successfully create your new lovestyle?

How do you expect your time alone together to change?

Do you think you'll be doing any new activities?

When you look at each other after the changes are made, what differences will you see?

Will either or both of you be saying different things?

Will your home be different in any way?

Will your jobs or careers be different?

Will the differences you notice be large or small?

What aspects of your relationship do you want to keep the same?

What aspects do you want to enhance or enlarge upon?

Make up some of your own questions, and when you've reached your conclusions, record them in your journal.

Exercise No. 4

One of the most effective things you can do to ensure success is to celebrate these changes. Celebration draws your attention to your success and rewards your efforts. I don't believe you can sustain the effort to achieve your goals without periodically appreciating how far you've come.

My colleague, Floyd Goff, describes this as a yardstick, stretching back into your past. If you count only the last few inches on the yardstick, you'll become easily discouraged, but if you periodically sight along its entire length, back to where you started, you'll be encouraged and energized.

To better understand this, review the instructions in Section I, "New Relationships," Exercise 4. Holidays are times when we're "supposed" to celebrate. Some of us have more experience and success at creating a feeling of appreciation, joy and special commemoration at these times. As a beginning toward creating new ways to celebrate, review the current celebrations in your life together.

What things do you really feel like celebrating? Richard and I toast major events with the crystal champagne "bride-and-groom" glasses we were given to use at our wedding. The minute those glasses come out, even if they're only full of ginger ale, the event becomes a major celebration.

What have you done that doesn't work? Many clients, upon reviewing holidays, realize that many of the "traditional" things done in their families were boring, or even unkind and painful for them. Upon review, do you find that your holiday "celebrations" are either grueling work, or that **much of the time is spent bickering or gossiping?**

Have you looked forward to the holiday with anticipation? When it's over, do you feel satisfied that your celebration was meaningful? As you discuss this, remember there are really no "rules" that can't be changed; you're only discussing what hasn't worked so you can correct it. Do you feel "burdened" by the cost of gift-giving and celebrating, or do you enjoy every moment of it? This discussion will enable you to distill the elements of celebration out of past events since you've been together, and before you met.

Once you've done that, make a list of what constitutes a celebration and what feels appropriate and satisfying to you. Then add to the list your fantasies of celebrations you've seen in movies and TV, read about in books, heard that other families do, etc. What would you like to try from those options? (Remember, usually you won't know if it will really satisfy you until you actually try it, but you can put it on your list of things to experiment with.)

One of my clients told me of a family Christmas ritual in which everyone old enough to talk, one at a time, reviewed their year and spoke of what they were grateful for and what they wished to change. Then they spoke directly to each other about what important interactions they'd had during the year. This was always taped, and my client told me how moving it was to listen to past tapes of her grandmother, who had recently died. I decided I wanted to add that ritual to my own celebrations, and made some personal modifications in it. Now it adds to my holiday joy, too.

Each of you will probably have different ideas. That's OK. Suzi and Ben, workshop attendees (strangers to each other), ran into a block doing a brief version of this exercise about birthdays. Their assignment was to plan a birthday celebration for each of them that would satisfy both. Suzi wanted to have a planned, organized celebration, but wanted to be surprised. Ben wanted to be spontaneous and do what he was moved to do at the time.

They thought they were at a stalemate, until I suggested that Ben could arrange for a friend who enjoyed giving parties to set up the surprise, and Ben's part could be to keep Suzi occupied (in spontaneous ways) until time for the party. I offered that as only one option of many they could use to break the stalemate, but they both thought it was a great idea, and the problem was solved.

You'll find, as Suzi and Ben did, that solutions can usually be found quite easily when you're willing to consider all your resources and options. The options aren't limited, only the thinking is. Friends are part of your resources, and can supply needs you're not willing or able to meet for each other. This exercise can be powerful, for it's the beginning of learning how to synthesize new styles out of old options.

CHAPTER TWO

CREATING COMMUNICATION: SHARING LOVESTYLES EFFECTIVELY

THE MOST EFFECTIVE COMMUNICATION skills are learning to take the time and space to *talk* about who you are and how you feel, and being interested in *hearing* about your partner's feelings and thoughts.

Communication is as simple as that. What get in the way of being effective are our assumptions, expectations, panic and anger. When I assume I know what you're thinking or how you're feeling without checking it out, I run a high risk of being wrong, acting on my wrong assumptions (thereby confusing you) and then totally misunderstanding your response to me.

Here's an important secret about the art of relating: Relationships are probably 85% response. That is:

I do or say something. (Stimulus)
You answer or react. (Response)
I then answer or react to you. (Response)
You then respond to my response. (Response)
I respond to your response to my response. (Response)
And so on.

In this whole sequence, there's only one stimulus (initial words or action) but many responses. The responses continue until someone changes the topic, or ends the series.

The important thing about this is that the one in the relationship who pays attention to his/her responses and initial actions or words (stimulus) can, by giving the other person something different, change the other's probable response. It's like the old saying, "You get more flies with honey than with vinegar."

How would you feel if you walked into a room and someone (obviously disappointed), said, "Oh. It's only you." What if his/her face lit up and he/she said, "Hi! How nice to see you!" Which greeting would get the best response from you? Thoughtful people know this and use it accordingly. If you need to solve a problem with your mate, the proper presentation of the problem can help you reach a mutually satisfying goal.

Many people who attend my lectures, workshops and one-by-one or couple counseling sessions are shocked by this idea, because they see it as "manipulation" and they see manipulation as wrong. I define manipulation as overpowering someone or coercing him/her through untruths and misstatements to do what he/she doesn't want to do. Manipulation implies that the other person is not free to make a decision based on the facts, either because facts are altered or withheld, or because he/she is forcibly prevented from choosing.

There's a great difference between coercing your partner and choosing your own actions based on the likelihood of success. Talking calmly and rationally, even when you're upset, because you know you'll be heard better by your mate, is no more insidious than wearing a "dress-for-success" outfit to a job interview. Both decisions are designed to give you a better chance at success.

We're about to explore some techniques for increasing the chances for success in your relationships: success in creating a relationship that meets the needs of both partners, and success in communicating effectively with your mate.

The exercises "For Individuals" are aimed at people who have not yet found their partners and those who have partners but are doing the exercises independently. The remainder of you will find it helpful to read them; there are bound to be times when you're having problems understanding each other, and these individual techniques can help.

The exercises in this chapter are a combination of techniques for communicating your lovestyle individually and helping your partner communicate with you. The two procedures cannot effectively be separated, since healthy communication involves both people sharing in a balanced way.

SECTION I

SHARING, HEARING, KEEPING THE BALANCE

Several years ago, Renee, a client who was working on the problem of encouraging a lover to open up, said, "Oh, I get it. It's like sharing your half of the sandwich first!"

Upon being asked to explain, she said that as a child in school she had learned that if another child had a sandwich she coveted, she had a better chance of "striking a deal" to trade or share if she offered to share her sandwich first.

Renee was right. Often, we wait for "clues" from the other person before taking a step into uncharted territory. So it follows that making a gentle, inviting first step is often all you need to assure success.

Also, it's important to be aware that, along with the advent of a new social consciousness about feminism and humanism, and with new "unisex" attitudes about jobs and social activities, there is also new confusion about sex roles, etiquette and social propriety. This confusion occurs among generally thoughtful and caring people who are concerned about giving offense.

Naturally, these are the people you would most like to have as your friends, and you'll find it useful to take the initiative in putting others at ease about what topics are OK for discussion.

A big problem people run into is the struggle that occurs when one person attempts to "push" another into a particular pattern that he/she has learned is the "right" way to relate. It's much more effective, especially if you're looking for a mate, to "follow" the relationship and see how it develops. Even in established relationships, you'll find a profound change occurs when you begin to recognize the patterns that have already been established and learn how to help them flow where you want them to instead of struggling against them.

There is a natural pattern which social interactions follow, and with a minor amount of knowledge and a bit of patience, you can learn to use that pattern to your distinct advantage. I see the pattern as a series of branching lines, like this:

```
            Y
          /   \
       Yes     No
      /   \
    No     Yes
          /   \
       Yes     No
      /   \
    No     Yes
```

Point "Y" is the beginning. From there you see branches, like a flowchart. Each branch has a "Yes" fork and a "No" fork. The "Yes"'s continue on to the next branch, while the "No"'s end. That's how a conversation between two people who have just met can be diagrammed. If A says "Hello," and B ignores it, B has just said "no" to further conversation. That's a "No" response, which dead-ends the conversation there, unless A is brave or foolhardy enough to begin again.

If, on the other hand, B says, "Hi, how are you?," that's an invitation to A to move to the next level, which may be, "Do you come here often?" or a comment on the evening, or any one of a thousand possible responses. That's a "Yes" response, which leads to the next possibility, and so on, until a "No" response appears on one side or the other.

Depending on the adroitness with which the two toss the conversational ball back and forth, they begin to get to know each other and to form impressions. These impressions are the result of unconsciously looking *back* at the "path" of the conversation (and eventually the hours, days, weeks, months, years spent together) and evaluating the quality of the interaction.

Please note that you can't decide effectively about whether

the relationship is succeeding or not by gazing *forward* into what "might happen" between you. That's a fantasy, and while fantasy can be fun and very useful as a guideline for choosing your directions, it's a terrible way to gauge whether or not what's going on *now* is working for you.

When looking for a partner with whom to share your life, it's *essential* that you pay attention to what's actually happening *now* and whether or not it's working *now*. Ignoring reality by covering it over with a pretty fantasy is ineffective and in the worst cases, dangerous. Being caught up in fantasy is what allows people to be confused, frustrated, ripped off, even brutalized and otherwise mistreated by mates, yet keep coming back for more.

There's a wonderful process I call "self-selection" that happens with people. Many people see only one side of it and call it "rejection," as in "I can't stand any more rejection; I'm giving up looking for a mate."

The *whole* process works like this: the more you allow yourself to be who you really are around others, to let your personality show, warts and all, the more people will self-select around you. That is, those who enjoy your personality will come closer, and those who don't will move away. Also, people will select certain aspects of your interaction to encourage and others to avoid.

This is a great time-and-energy saver, because it keeps you from getting in too deep with people with whom you must keep up false appearances. You can never get very close to people who require you to keep up a facade; it's too stressful. So those who self-select away from you are doing themselves *and* you a favor, saving you both time and energy.

Out of those who have selected toward you, you're now free to conduct your *own* selection process, based on the "Yes/No" diagram we've already discussed.

To recap, what I refer to as "following the relationship," or "letting the relationship guide you," consists of two major tools:

(1) Learning to be comfortable enough with yourself to let others know who you really are, so that the self-selection process can occur on a realistic basis.

(2) Paying close attention to what has been happening between you, so that you have concrete, solid information about how to make your choice.

As Sonya Friedman says in her wonderful book, *Men Are Just Desserts* (Warner Books, 1983): "In the early stages of courtship, romance is dazzling. When you think you're falling in love, your vision blurs and you develop selective hearing. To your slightly malfunctioning senses, reality is distorted. You see what you want to see and hear what you need to hear. What happens? You miss the clues that are laid out before you. A man reveals himself very early in the relationship, and you need all your faculties to be attuned to him." (A secret, men: it's the same for you as it is for women; in fact, I find Ms. Friedman's book as effective for men as for women.)

No matter what your situation is, single or coupled, long-term or just beginning, knowing how to see the signs and interpret correctly who your partner is will help make you a master of the art of relationships.

EXERCISES FOR INDIVIDUALS

Keeping these ideas in mind, let's move on to some practical ways of finding a potential mate and getting him/her to reveal his/her lovestyle, so you can make a rational, informed decision.

For those of you who have mates, but experience dissatisfaction sometimes, the following exercises will help you discover what satisfaction is available from him/her, and help you find other sources, if necessary, for getting everything you want.

Exercise No. 1

In the last section, we set up a plan to find compatible people, both as friends and potential partners. It's very important for you to follow through on that process until you have a sufficient network of people in your life.

While you're doing that, however, you can also be working through the people you already know to practice your research. Beginning today, observe your friends, family, co-workers, etc., in a new way.

I've heard it said that each of us is only three people away from the President of the United States. This means that if you comb through your friends, their friends and their friends' friends, you'll find a chain of three people who connect in such a way that the third person will personally know the President. This impressed me because it's true for me. There's actually only one other person between me and the President, because I happen to have a friend who works in Congress. Check it out for yourself: if you have a friend of yours introduce you to a friend of his/hers, and that friend introduces you to his/her friend, how many links would it take to connect you to the White House?

This seems silly, I know, but it illustrates an important point. With the same sort of network of friends and friends of friends, you could arrange to meet the most eligible potential partner you could think of. Even your favorite movie star!

So start using that valuable network of people you know. Make closer friends of your acquaintances and co-workers. Don't reject someone as a friend because they're married, the wrong sex or otherwise ineligible. Everyone you know has friends! One of those friends just might be the perfect friend for you—or the perfect mate!

Everyone who is in a relationship (and even some who aren't) is eager to do matchmaking. Our friend Ed, who brought me to the party where I met Richard, has brought so many people together, he's known to his friends as "Cupid." When Richard and I first met, we were astounded to realize how many people we both knew without ever meeting each other! Whether you're aware of it or not, you probably know people like our friend Ed. Keep your eyes open. Don't be afraid to let people know you're looking.

These resources work equally well in finding other partners with whom to do specific activities your main partner is reluctant to participate in. For example, one of the best ways to communicate your desire for more exercise is to get a tennis partner and play regularly. Who knows, if your mate sees you enjoying this, he/she may want to join in! At least, you've removed the struggle over the activity from your relationship.

In your journal, describe your current network and make some notes about how you can expand it. You may also want to consider some of the "links" you have to people you thought would be impossible to meet, and how to get yourself introduced to them or to the people who know them.

Exercise No. 2

Once you find new people, you need to have an effective process for proceeding. No matter who you meet or what you're doing, you're now in a position to start "testing" for compatibility.

In a long-standing relationship, you're not really testing for compatibility, you're finding out more about someone you already know.

It's simple if you *pay attention*! People give countless clues about who they are, what they like and don't like, how they view life, how successful they feel and how they define it. Most of the clues are not contained in what they're saying, but in how they act and in inferences you can make about them from their lifestyles, mannerisms, etc.

Most of us would love to talk about ourselves, but are reluctant to, afraid others aren't interested. Merely showing interest in another person's life and opinions can be enough to open the floodgates and allow him/her to feel comfortable sharing.

The art of conversation lies in asking questions without appearing to interrogate the other person. There are numerous examples of this process in movies, TV, plays and books. Making a statement about yourself, followed by a leading question, can be an effective way of doing this. For example:

You: "I feel a little awkward at this party. The only person I know is Jane, who brought me. Do you know many people here?"

He/she: "Yes, Ted, who lives here, has been my friend for a long time. [Aha! Long friendship—good sign!] I know most of the people here."

You: "Wonderful! Maybe you can help me get to know some of them."

He/she: "Who would you like to meet?"

You: "I'd like to begin by getting to know you. I'm enjoying this conversation and this party. Does Ted throw parties like this often?"

By this time, your conversation is off to a great start, and you've laid the groundwork for it to continue long enough to find out what you want to know. Darlene, a client who originally came to me for help in ending a problem relationship and to learn how to find compatible men, calls this process "screening." She says it made her dating much more fun, and she was amazed at how much she could learn about people in a short time. (Darlene is getting married this year.)

Often, people with longterm spouses who come to me for counseling are amazed at how easily a normally reticent person will talk to me. This has been true with an eleven-year-old boy, as well as with many adults of both sexes. I use the technique just demonstrated, coupled with giving the person plenty of time to answer. If you're in a longterm relationship, you'll be surprised how effective it is to show the same interest in your partner that you'd show in a new friend. The same techniques for "screening" also work for getting to know an old friend better.

Knowing what information you want is essential to effective information-gathering. There are many ways of finding out whether you and your new friend have enough in common to continue exploring the friendship; or whether you and your old friend can generate some new energy. The point is, if you direct the conversation to what most concerns you, you'll find out very soon what the possibilities are.

Here's an example: One night after giving a lecture, when I knew Richard wasn't home and I felt the need to "wind down," I went to a local hotel bar to relax for a while before driving home. There were many friendly people there, and a group of men from a convention started talking to me. I had a long, delightful conversation with one of them. Had I been looking for a relationship, this would have been an opportunity—so, just for fun, I checked him out.

In ten minutes, I knew he and I would not do well together, in spite of how easily we talked. Once we had exhausted work and our respective cities as conversation, the only other thing he could or would talk about was sports. The man was a sports fanatic, and when I asked how he spent his time, he said he spent every weekend watching sports on TV during the day.

Since I'm not a sports enthusiast and don't watch TV much, he and I would have had a major problem before we even started. Not much point in going beyond that conversation!

In case this sounds like I'm too picky, keep in mind that it's a matter of degree. Someone who likes sports from time to time might bring a new dimension of fun into my life, but someone for whom sports are of major importance as a recreational pastime just wouldn't work for me.

His lack of interest in political, social, philosophical or literary topics was a major block for me. There were also other clues about his interests that told me we had little in common. Perhaps if he had been interested in the psychology and philosophy of sports, or even in sports as a political metaphor, I might have wanted to learn from him and been interested enough to pursue the relationship further.

Once I had the information, it was simple to drop hints that I was unavailable and uninterested in future contact, and the conversation ended pleasantly, on a friendly basis. I believe we both felt good about the time spent with each other, simply for the entertainment value.

On the other hand, when I met my dear friend Sylvia, Richard and I were out dancing. She and her partner complimented us, and we began to talk. In just a few minutes, between dances, I knew Sylvia and I had both professional and other interests in common.

At that time, I was new to my city and felt the need of local friends, since my long-time friends were all forty-five and fifty miles away. My feeling of isolation was putting too much pressure on me and my relationships. So, realizing Sylvia had potential, I immediately said, "I'm new to Long Beach and looking for new friends in town. Are you available for lunch some day this week?" We took out our calendars on the spot and made a date. Five years later, we're still friends.

To give yourself the best possible chance of success, formulate a series of questions designed to gather information subtly and quickly. Base your questions on your ideal lifestyle, developed in the previous exercises. Be clear whether you're looking for a friend or mate, or exploring possibilities with an existing mate. You'll need specific questions tailored to each situation, although many questions will work for all three. Note these questions and variations in your book.

Experiment with different ways to introduce these topics into your conversation, and subtle ways to ask your questions. Practice in front of your mirror and whenever you get a chance for conversation.

Exercise No. 3

Whether your relationship is long-standing, new or still a dream, ponder what you most want your significant partner to know about you. For example, you may decide that you want him/her to know that you're really more sensitive than you appear to be; or that you have a great sense of humor that takes a while to come out.

Consider revealing that important information about yourself. Even new people in your lfe can learn about you right away. Remember, the easier it is for someone to see who you really are, the easier it is for him/her to successfully relate to you.

Experiment with saying out loud (when you're alone): "What I want you to know about me is. . . ." and complete the sentence. After you're comfortable with that, experiment with gently adding it to your conversation.

This is a technique in the "art" of relating. It takes practice and skill to become good at it. Take it easy, go slowly and have fun with it. The point is not to hit someone with it as though it were a sledgehammer, but to offer it as a bit of light on the mystery of who you are.

Balancing that with your interest in who the other person is will keep a nice easy flow. Remember to go for balance, alternating your sharing with your partner's, and encouraging your partner to share often.

If you like, you can put this information in the form of a "confession": "I've been embarrassed to tell you this, but ..." Or a fantasy: "I've always dreamed of ..." Or casual conversation: "Do you know what I'd like right now ... ?" It's also very effective to follow your disclosure with a question about your partner. "Have you ever felt like that?" "What would you like most?" Or even, "Do you think that's silly (greedy, childish) of me?"

While you're trying these techniques, remember to keep the conversational ball bouncing. As you learn more, write the results of your experiments in your book and build on them.

Exercise No. 4

Having made your new friend, you'll soon be faced with the question of what to share as your relationship with him/her deepens (even longterm ones will deepen with this kind of mutual disclosure). Once you begin an atmosphere of mutual sharing, you have only to maintain that process. Each of you has a right to your privacy, and remember that there is an inverse ratio between the degree of privacy and the degree of intimacy you feel. (That is, the more privacy, the less intimacy, and vice versa.)

The most effective thing you can do to ensure your success is to keep the sharing as nearly equal as you can. Since it never works to push someone else, the best way to keep things equal is to slow down if you find you're doing most of the sharing. You may be going too fast for the other person, and he/she may not be able to get a word in edgewise.

If you're not able to slow down your rate of sharing or making contact to match the other person's, then the relationship is probably not workable, or will take more effort than you're willing to expend.

One way or another, you'll eventually get to the place at which I find most of my clients' confusion arises: sharing feelings about sex and sexuality. When you want to keep a relationship at the level of friendship, handle the topic of sex early.

Difficult as it may be to believe in today's atmosphere of sexual revolution/hype and accompanying backlash, sex is just another form of human interaction and follows the same protocol as other forms of intercourse. However, because social convention has sensitized us to our sexuality, we tend to be less forgiving of ourselves and others in matters of sexual expression.

Therefore, there's a need to be gentle with yourself and others—it's a tender area. When you have some feeling or need to share, and you're nervous about it, just say so. "I'd like to ask (tell) you something, but I'm embarrassed (scared, shy)." Or, "I want to tell you something, but I'm afraid I'll hurt your feelings."

If you've picked an appropriate time, this will probably put your partner in his/her most accepting, noncritical mood, and you'll be encouraged to go ahead and say it.

The most effective thing you can do to encourage the smooth flow of communication between you is also the simplest: *Pay attention to your partner!* The other person will consistently and constantly give you signals about whether or not the conversation feels comfortable.

If you're talking, and your companion gets a glazed look, perhaps you're monopolizing the conversation, or have chosen an uncomfortable or boring topic. As soon as you notice this, ask a question to get your partner to choose a new topic he/she finds more interesting.

For those of you who talk easily, remember, when dealing with a less verbal person, don't overwhelm him/her with ideas. Express one simple idea at a time, and give your companion a chance to respond. In other words, make sure he/she can get a "word in edgewise."

If you are the one whose mind is wandering, check out why your companion might be out of touch. Is he/she showing signs of nervousness that might keep him/her talking non-stop? If you guess this is so, say something reassuring or complimentary and see if it helps. Or bring up a topic that's of more interest to you.

Experiment with each new person you meet (and with your partner, if you already have a relationship) and keep a record in your book of what works. If you know that your evening goes better when you have an activity rather than a whole evening of conversation, you have an advantage in deciding what to do. When you realize your partner is on an earlier schedule and falls asleep by 11:00 P.M., while you can stay up longer, you can adjust your date accordingly and not waste time early in the evening.

Your careful observations and notes (made when you're alone!) will give you real clues about what works with each new friend (or with your partner), and from these clues you can decide rather quickly what a longterm relationship will require.

At worst, with a new person you can easily see that life with him/her would be an unending struggle at communication, and decide to keep looking, rather than pressure each other until you're both angry and frustrated. Worst case with an established partner is that you'll see communication is seriously damaged and be able to get help. If you're not experiencing some improvement by now (or at least feeling more hopeful), counseling is in order. Go now, before things get worse.

At best, you'll have a clear idea of how well you'll do together, and you'll get closer quickly. Before long, your experience will tell you that you have a "relationship" instead of just an unknown quantity in your life. Your partner will become used to communicating, and you can begin using the techniques for new relationships.

EXERCISES FOR NEW RELATIONSHIPS

By doing the Chapter 1 exercises together, you've already done much of the work toward communicating. The emphasis here is on the importance of "following," rather than leading or pushing your relationship through its development, as I explained at the beginning of this section.

It's impossible to have a relationship as the person you would *like* to be, or with your beloved's "potential" or "better self." Your relationship must be designed to work for both of you *now*, warts and all.

The most important prerequisite for success is to get to know the person you're with, and to reveal the "real" you as much as you can. Only when you're dealing with reality and truth can you express your love *effectively*.

Often I see people in love attempting to pressure each other or themselves to change into someone easier to handle. I've never yet seen it work. If you're a person who wants and needs sexual freedom, for example, being told the one you love "can't stand" openness will usually only tempt you to lie and sneak.

Hiding who you are, or being unwilling to see the person you love clearly, is not wrong—it's just that it's impossible to build any trust or security under those conditions. So the following exercises are designed to aid you in discovering the truth. You may not like everything you learn. That's OK.

We seldom like every aspect of ourselves, let alone others. It isn't necessary that you like all aspects of a person for you to effectively and successfully love him/her. I believe it's necessary to respect and value each other, but not to like everything that's said and done.

In fact, there have been many times when I've counseled a client to do something that strongly angered his/her spouse at first. However, the increased level of respect my client earned actually raised his/her value in the eyes of the mate, creating an increased sense of my client's worth as a person and a partner.

There are times when the truth hurts, but if it's shared without malice, it usually results in greater intimacy after the upset passes. Truth really does set us free.

Take your time, go easy on yourself and your partner, and remember your objective: a relationship that really works for both of you.

Exercise No. 1

Some of the most powerful information you can obtain from a partner is what happened in past relationships. Find a quiet moment together and discuss your past. When you let each other know that you care and are sympathetic, you'll find that the information will most likely come tumbling out.

Of all the people who are my clients, even the reluctant ones (usually three or four new clients come to me each week), I've *never* had anyone refuse to tell me about themselves. This isn't some magical attribute of my California Counseling License, it's a response to my obvious caring about people and my lack of judgmental response. Many new clients tell me they've never been able to talk about themselves before and they're surprised how easy it is to talk to me. Strangers used to tell me their problems long before I was a counselor. (This was one of the factors that encouraged me to get my license.)

The same skills that make it easy for strangers to open up to me will make it easy for you to communicate with each other.

Before you begin to do this, you *must* decide you're willing to hear the truth and suspend criticism. Also, you're *not* doing this so you can give advice. You're asking for information in order to learn. Your objective is to get to know each other better, warts and all. You'll be learning each other's past patterns, so you can use the information to express your love more effectively. The knowledge will help you think more clearly when problems arise between you, and recognize potential problems before they become factors in your relationship.

It's not difficult to be receptive and understanding if you remember not to take your beloved's past personally. It happened before you arrived, and it has very little to do with you. It's merely history, and like all history, it can present patterns that are useful to observe.

If learning the truth is too difficult for you, stop here. Get yourself some help, if you want to continue. If you do go on, and a particular secret you learn turns out to be difficult to take, recognize the difficulty as your own problem and get some professional advice.

During this sharing, identify out loud with what you're told as much as you can. Responses like "I know how that feels —it happened to me once"; or, "Wow, that must have been tough," let the other person know you understand, and aren't judging. Keep your responses brief, so you don't interrupt the flow of the story.

Avoid "Why didn't you tell her off?" or, "You should (shouldn't) have said that." These responses will shut off the flow of communication instantly, because they sound critical.

Above all, don't push. If you're asking a question and you get a one-syllable reply, back off a bit. At that point you can offer to share your experience instead. Say, "It's hard to talk about, isn't it? I know my divorce is—but I want you to know about that part of my life, too." Don't overdo it and wind up monopolizing the conversation—just share one or two details, then allow your partner to respond with some of his/her own experiences.

If a past relationship was very difficult, the discussion may slow down, but if you show that you're interested, aren't going to judge and are willing to share your experience too, the talk will soon flow easily.

Often clients have said to me, "I don't communicate very well." My response usually is, "I understand every word so far, and I don't find it hard to talk to you." As soon as I say that, the client relaxes and really begins to share.

Most people who have been told they don't communicate well have just run into someone with a different style, who was convinced his/her way was the *only* way. Consequently, they've been intimidated and criticized into believing they don't do it "right." The truth may be that they've been frightened out of doing it *at all!*

It's almost impossible to survive on this planet without some ability to communicate. Most of us do it fine—for the environment in which we spend most of our time. It's only when we feel afraid of making a mistake that we get nervous, forget what we know and stop thinking. No one can communicate under that kind of stress.

To encourage each other to open up, realize that your partner may have a different style or set of rules about communication than you do. For example, some of your communication may be nonverbal—gestures, sounds, facial expressions—but this may not be your partner's style at all. Being willing to listen to your partner's style *as it is* will go a long way toward solving the problem and helping both of you relax.

Also, it can help to set a time and place that makes it easy to talk.

Don't try to talk intimately if you're in danger of being over-heard or interrupted frequently.

Find a comfortable place to be—comfortable chairs, a soothing atmosphere.

Set a regular time together that's just for communication—don't be so physically active or so busy that there's never any time.

Give lots of little "rewards" to each other for communication: Say how much you're enjoying the talk, hold hands, encourage each other, etc.

Be aware of the "balance" of your conversation: share more of yourself if you feel your partner has shared a lot, and hold back a little when you feel you've shared more.

As you find out what works for the two of you, make notes in your book about what's effective, to remind yourself what to do more often. Also make notes about what you learn.

Here's how this has worked for me: Before I married Richard, I learned that the most frustrating thing to him in several relationships was people who had fallen asleep on him when he was feeling romantic. I made a mental note, and sure enough, a few months later I began to get sleepy just as he was feeling romantic.

That set off an "alarm" in my mind, and I began to look for a reason why. I found he was "procrastinating" about lovemaking, doing little odd jobs and projects around the house just before bed. We talked about it and discovered he thought he had to stay in bed once we made love, and he wasn't tired enough yet.

The solution was easy. We realized we could make love early, then he could get up again and take some time for himself to do projects, etc. It worked like a charm.

Now we can laugh about it. He says, after we make love and then relax for a while, "I have to get up now and run around the block." And we both laugh. Now I get to be romantic before I'm too tired, and he isn't angry about me falling asleep. All because I found out what had gone wrong in his past relationships.

It's worth your time and patience to find out about the past. It can make a big difference in your future.

Exercise No. 2

Another important part of your histories to discuss is childhood. This works the same way. Ask some simple, gentle questions and don't judge the answers. Find out about each other's brothers and/or sisters. If you've met them, ask what they were like then as compared to now. If not, simply tell each other stories about childhood.

Go back over some of the earlier exercises you did and ask some of those questions about holidays, about whether home felt loving or not, etc. Sensitivity and gentle mutual interest are important here. Avoid mutual interrogation.

Don't get off balance and ask questions as though you're interviewing a job applicant. If either of you balks, clams up or fidgets, that's nonverbal communication. Be sensitive enough to realize you're probably coming on too strong. Remember, focus on the balance, and share more or less of your own story according to how things are going.

As you talk, you can monitor your effect by your partner's reaction. If you're paying attention, you can see your approach reflected in your companion's responses and adjust your presentation for best effect. If you consistently get a poor response, have a friend check out your manner, or see a counselor for help. Sometimes we need lessons in grace and style.

Actually, heavy instructions aside, this is a fun process. We've all told childhood stories before. The only difference here is your intent to learn. Both of you will enjoy it and feel enriched. Record essential information in your book for future reference.

Exercise No. 3

Just as in Exercises 1 and 2, find gentle, subtle ways to discuss your "ideal relationship." Ask each other questions like the following, allowing plenty of time for response and discussion:

If we could have a perfect relationship, what would it be like for you?

What activities would we do together, what would you do separately?

How much time would we spend together, how much alone?

What have you always wished you could do in a relationship that you have never achieved?

What scares you most about relationships? Commitment? Marriage?

As always, I have some cautionary words. In addition to being careful not to sound like Grand Inquisitors, continue to make sure you're not taking the answers personally. Yes, you are drawing each other out so you can see the possibilities, but you're only fantasizing, not under oath. Fantasies can be fantastic—that is, inaccurate. What you dream you'd like may not match reality.

I'm reminded of the scene in the movie *Tootsie* in which Dustin Hoffman, impersonating a woman, is told by the woman he loves that she wishes men were more honest, and she'd love it if someone would say directly that he's attracted to her and would like to take her to bed. Later, at a cocktail party where he goes as a man, Hoffman sees her and follows her wishes to the letter (using the "inside information" he got as a "woman"). She throws a drink in his face. My point is: We don't always know accurately what we want, and what we want at this moment may not be what we want tomorrow.

The key here is flexibility. This information is valuable and useful, *provided you're thinking clearly and using it thoughtfully*. It's a guideline, a starting point—not a rigid, inflexible rule. By paying attention to each other's nonverbal signals, you can tell how to proceed. Take your time, and record your discoveries in your book.

Exercise No. 4

This is a discussion of your feelings about each other right now. You'll be asking for a little more personal disclosure, and it may feel a little more risky to both of you.

Then again, it can be very exhilarating and exciting. As always, your guideline is: Are we both having fun? If not, drop it for now—never make hard work out of it, and if you find it becoming a burden, *stop*. Lighten up the atmosphere, find a way to have fun and come back to this exercise another time. You won't get where you want to go unless the journey is pleasurable.

Here are some typical questions to start you off:

How do you feel about our relationship so far? ("So, how do you like it so far?" is a humorous way Richard and I ask this.)

What would you change about our relationship if you could?

Would you add anything new? What?

Is there anything you'd like to try with me that you haven't yet? What is it?

I don't understand what's going on with us right now—do you?

What we're doing right now feels (funny, great, awful, strange, etc.) to me. How does it feel to you?

What do you like best about being with me?

What do you like least about being with me?

Let this be funny and silly as well as serious. Some of these questions are a great way to get playful with your sexuality. Pay close attention to the answers and take it slow. You have years to find out all the answers—all you want to do now is make a beginning.

As you do this exercise, also be aware of your feelings about what's happening right now. Give each other feedback about communication styles. For example, you could say, "I'm not getting a chance to complete my thought before you say something. Please go a little slower." Or, "I'm concerned that I may be talking too much—is there something you want to say?"

It's also possible to ask for the type of feedback you want *before* you share. You can say, "This is hard for me to say, so I'd like you to just listen and not say anything. Please just hold my hand."

Once you've gotten here, you may be in a place where you want to do the longterm exercises in this book together. Or you may have learned the attitudes and techniques well enough so that you don't need any more. At any rate, by doing this gently and slowly, before too long you'll reach a place where your communication is coming naturally and easily.

Keep recording what you learn, and return to it from time to time to check your focus.

If you're at this point, have done everything up to here *slowly* and *gently*, and yet still feel frustrated by your lack of communication, it's time to seek help. See a counselor, by yourself or together. Richard and I go from time to time, because we find our counselor makes it easier to solve sticky issues, and we feel we deserve the help. Getting counseling for your problems early can help you solve them simply and easily, before you build up resentment and frustration. One or two sessions now can save you six months of heavy sessions later.

Books and classes can be very helpful, but there's nothing like the personal, individualized attention you can get from a real live counselor. Shop around until you find one who feels good to you.

EXERCISES FOR LONGTERM RELATIONSHIPS

By doing the Chapters 1 and 2 exercises together, either as a new relationship or an established one, you've already done much of the work toward communicating.

In a longterm association, habit patterns are created, some of which are healthy (they work) and some of which are not (they lead to dissatisfaction and/or confusion).

People in brand-new relationships need to learn how to communicate effectively. But as a couple with established patterns, you may not only need to learn how to communicate with each other, you may need to correct some old patterns which aren't working for you.

Gentleness and patience are important here. Of course, you want things to go smoothly between you. Of course, you're anxious to do well, and to do it right away. However, the most effective way to fix relationship issues is to go slowly and gently, making sure the wants and needs of *both* partners are considered.

These exercises will help you avoid the problems which arise when you're sending messages that say, "Be reasonable—do it *my* way." In *How to Be a Couple and Still Be*

Free, Riley and I outlined a problem-solving process which is effective and successful. If you have trouble with the following, refer back to that process for help.

If you run into serious difficulty, please do yourself the favor of getting some assistance. An independent, emotionally detached viewpoint can be tremendously beneficial. An experienced counselor can help you repair old damage without creating new problems.

Lest that dire warning frighten you, let me assure you that these exercises were designed to feel good and be fun. If your relationship is basically in good shape and just needs some wrinkles ironed out, or if there aren't any serious wrinkles, and you just want to explore more deeply, this will be fun and rewarding.

Exercise No. 1

Probably the most important thing you can do to encourage communication is to "set the scene" or create an atmosphere which allows conversation to flow easily. Many of us have no difficulty communicating when we have enough time. The best "flow-starter" I know is genuine interest on the part of the listener.

Often, with business, children and the other pressures and distractions of life, we forget that we need time together. Many parents get so involved with their children that they forget that they also have a relationship that needs nurturing. Since parents' most effective tool is role modeling, the health of your relationship is important to your children, too.

I'm reminded of the saying, "Why is there always enough time to do it over, but never enough time to do it right?"

Taking sufficient time to communicate now saves incredible amounts of time and energy later, because it forestalls confusion, struggle and fights.

So, take some time now and look around your house or apartment. Is there a good setting for communication? When you do talk, where do you do it? Is it in a comfortable place that will allow you to relax and take your time? Or is it in the kitchen, standing up, while someone's attention is really on dinner?

It's possible to have good talks while doing a chore together —making dinner, weeding in the garden, painting a wall— as long as you pay attention to how you *feel*. Are you rushed, annoyed at being interrupted? Are you feeling distracted, not wanting to be bothered with the conversation? If so, talking while doing chores is not working for you.

This is another one of the areas in which you're required to use your own judgment. I can only give you some guidelines to follow. The truth is, however, that if you begin to think in terms of allowing intimacy and conversation to take place, you'll know when you achieve a good atmosphere for them.

Make sure your living space contains areas that are comfortable for relaxed conversation: perhaps comfortable chairs in the privacy of your bedroom (especially if you have children), or moving the livingroom furniture closer together, is all you need.

Once there is an inviting physical area, all you need is the time. On a Friday night, don't go out for a change. If you have children, arrange to send them to a friend's house for the evening or overnight. Make it a quiet evening at home.

Or retire early to your bedroom and arrange not to be disturbed except for emergencies.

Dagmar O'Connor, in "Too Busy for Sex?" (*New Woman*, August 1985) says, "Of course, finding time alone in a busy household—especially if you have children—can be difficult. But it's not impossible; it just requires more planning. Rule One of any household with children is *put a lock on the bedroom door and use it.* You're not rejecting your children by doing this; you're simply creating your own privacy."

In your book, record your ideas about how to make more time for sharing. After examining your living space, list your ideas for making cosy conversation easier and more inviting. Discuss the need for more time together (gently, gently) and help each other with ideas and plans.

Perhaps you can make minor adjustments and look for times when you can "just happen" to spend some time alone together. It may be possible to have lunch together if you both work, or to meet somewhere after work on an afternoon for a snack or something to drink. It's easy to say, "I'm going to be near your work Tuesday. Can I take you out to lunch (or after work)?"

Richard and I reserve Friday evenings for being together. Sometimes work or a social engagement will interfere, but we always check with each other before giving Fridays away. It provides a time in our busy schedules when we can count on each other, when we can discuss whatever we haven't had time for all week, share our dreams and plans and just enjoy each other. I always look forward to it—even on those rare weeks when we've seen quite a bit of each other.

Be a little less quick to turn on the TV, or to get involved in a book or project, and you may find conversation easier.

Note your ideas in your book, and add to it as new options open.

Exercise No. 2

Once you've set the stage for conversation, have possible topics ready. Your shared past is an excellent choice. You can easily begin by discussing some pleasant memories. What's important here is to ask whether your partner remembers these events the same way you do. Make it clear that you're interested in each other's opinions, feelings, reactions, etc.

Take your time with this; please be careful not to make it oppressive or obnoxious. The object is to have an interesting discussion, not to feel forced to talk. It's not a question-and-answer session; there are no wrong answers or comments.

Once you've established a pleasant habit of quiet conversation, it will become easier and easier to find out more. Here are some suggestions for questions you can ask *once in a while* and *one at a time* during conversations. It may take many conversations to cover all of them.

What do you think of as our happiest time together? What made it special for you?

Do you remember the time you got so mad at me? (Give an example.) What could I have done to make it better at the time? Are you still angry? Is there anything I can do to fix it? (Be careful not to get defensive here—you're interested in each other's impression, not your own guilt or innocence.)

One of the times I felt most loved by you was . . . (Give an example.) Do you remember it? What were you feeling then?

Please don't whip out a list of questions and begin interrogating each other. The above questions are merely to give you a general idea about how to open up the topic of your relationship and your mutual reactions to it. Using these examples, come up with some questions of your own. Write them in your book and keep them in mind.

The opportunity to discuss these topics will definitely arise, and if you're paying attention, you'll know when it does. Allow some time to pass before broaching the next subject.

Record what you learn about creating new ways to talk intimately in your book.

Exercise No. 3

On a rainy afternoon, or a late morning in bed, have a "let's pretend" session. If you two could have anything you want, do anything you want, what would you do?

What sounds like the most wonderful day off you could imagine?

The most wonderful vacation?

The most wonderful Valentine's Day/Anniversary gift?

The best surprise you could have when you come home from work?

The nicest conversation?

Get the idea? It's OK if these flights of fancy are materialistic or silly or outrageous—you'll still get lots of information about your mate's wants, and he/she will get lots about yours.

One of my favorite fantasies is from the movie *Darling Lily*. The hero is wooing the lady, and he must have conspired with her maid, for the lady wakes up one morning in her own house, her own bed, and there is one yellow rose on her pillow. With it is a card: "One rose, one thought of you." Then she goes downstairs, and her entire house is filled with yellow roses! Now, *that's* my idea of a grand gesture!

I told Richard about that fantasy, and he has never gone to such an extravagance (thank goodness!), but he does bring me flowers frequently. He understands that flowers mean a lot to me.

This is the advantage of fantasy-out-loud. Encourage your partner to share fantasies with you, and then act on them in whatever way possible. If she wants a mink coat, maybe rabbit or fake fur would be affordable. Or even a furry teddy bear. If he wants a Jaguar or a Ferrari, maybe some racy driving gloves or a license-plate frame that says, "My other car is . . . " would make him smile. If the dreams are more sensual in nature, it costs nothing to playact a fantasy scene.

The important thing is that you let each other know that fantasies are OK, that you *do* listen and that you support each other's heart's desire as much as you can. Setting up an atmosphere of mutual acceptance and openness for sharing can lead to more spontaneity and more accurate and wonderful impulsive surprises.

One day, a dear male friend of mine figured out that flowers were important to me, and since we can talk about most anything, he confessed that he felt unsure and intimidated in florist shops. He didn't know what or how to order, and so he avoided them.

I explained that I considered a dozen red roses to be an extravagance, only to be sent on extravagant occasions. What would do equally well would be a spray of two or three flowers, with a little greenery. It was more the *idea* of getting flowers than the cost of the gift. I also explained that florists were usually friendly, understanding people who value customers who frequently send a few flowers as much as customers who occasionally send expensive arrangements.

On my next birthday, I received a dozen long-stemmed roses from that man. It definitely works to let people know what you like, and to find out their dreams, too. As you make discoveries, write them in your book, along with notations about what works best to encourage your partner to open up. You can explore these experiments for weeks and/or months, constantly learning new things and continually improving your openness and sharing between yourselves.

Exercise No. 4

Periodically check in with each other to see if your relationship might be completing a phase and need to be updated. Richard and I use our wedding-anniversary date for this process. We sit down shortly before the anniversary and discuss how we've felt about the previous year—what we'd like to change and what we're pleased about.

This is always a warm and enjoyable occasion for us, and we follow it up by renewing our vows on our anniversary. I'm always surprised by how creative and powerful our discussion is, because we usually begin it with mild embarrassment and some silliness. Still, once we get started, our association really benefits from our "state-of-the-union" conference.

If you'd like to do this, some of the topics you might discuss are:

Time spent together: enough, too rushed, too easily postponed or changed?

Financial status: income and investment goals for the next year, how you've done so far, whether your financial picture is going as planned or needs to be refocused.

Emotional climate: Are you mostly satisfied? Having enough fun? Sexually comfortable? (Some of this usually gets covered in the time-together issue.)

What do you want to bring into your relationship this year? (If there's an unresolved issue, this is a good time to agree to get counseling help.)

Other issues can be discussed, too. This can be a good time to set some material goals such as: major alterations to the house, deciding on your vacation for this year, education for one of you or the children.

This is only a guideline. Your topics for discussion must be *yours*. You'll probably find, as I do, that knowing you'll have this discussion each year helps keep you conscientious about handling small issues as they arise.

This is also not just a license to complain. Celebration is important here, too. Be very careful not to complain unless you have a solution to offer. The solution can be simply to seek out more options, to consult an expert or to ask each other's opinion. To criticize or complain without presenting a solution is too provocative and will lead to defensiveness or arguing. The requirement of having an alternative suggestion forces you to think constructively about the problem.

Record the final results of your discussion in your book, along with the format, if you like.

CHAPTER THREE

SYNTHESIZING LOVESTYLES

THE SYNTHESIS OF LOVESTYLES is the blending of individual styles into a compatible shared style. Therefore, this chapter only applies to persons already in a relationship; and the category "For Individuals" here applies only to persons who have partners but are doing the exercises by themselves. Singles may want to read them, too, for future use.

Here we'll be confronting belief systems that say "impossible" or "we can't have it both ways." The truth is you *can* "have your cake and eat it, too." All you need is two cakes.

If you believe that's too flip, stop and think for a moment. What it means is that with proper forethought and provision, it's quite easy to have what you want now and also be prepared for later. It may be true that you can't "make an omelet without breaking eggs," but they don't have to be the last two eggs in the world. If they were, wouldn't it make a lot more sense to hatch them and wait till the chickens lay more?

That is the essence of successful synthesis. It requires the willingness to *think* about the results of your actions, to plan ahead for success. I've heard many times that most people believe being that rational is "too hard"—but is it really any harder than the pain you can cause yourself by irresponsible, panicky behavior?

Synthesis will occur, whether you plan for it or not. Unplanned for, it can become exactly what you've feared most in relationships. Thought out carefully, it can become "having your cake and eating it, too," or having what you want without giving up what's dear to you.

You may indeed have to give up some cherished prejudices, some acting without thought, some of the habits that have never worked for you anyway—but never anything that truly harmonizes with your personal values. When you're willing to examine your wants enough to satisfy them effectively, you'll find satisfaction easy to achieve—not only for you, but also for your partner.

Section I

THE NITTY GRITTY: WHAT YOU WANT/NEED IN YOUR RELATIONSHIP; YOUR ESSENTIAL INDIVIDUALITY OF STYLE

In this section, you'll get a chance to examine your cherished desires, the main reasons you're in a relationship to begin with. What is it you want? What does your partner want? What are the key factors in loving and being loved?

What ingredients are there that would cause you to think, "If I can't have that, I don't want a relationship at all"? What's your "bottom line"? Synthesis starts here, and the issue is: "How can you and I work it out so the most important ingredients for each of us are included?"

Most of these combinations of important wants can be worked out. What keeps us "stuck" are our imaginary rules for how it "should" be. Whenever you can relax your rules, you'll find that your options increase, and solving the problem gets easier.

Often, just clarifying your wants and getting a clear look at your different lovestyles will help suggest a solution. Sometimes we panic and decide "It's all over, there's nothing that will solve this." A cool, calm evaluation of the situation can be tremendously helpful. Counselors and therapists often appear very wise about problems, mainly because they can see the situation calmly and think clearly. After all, your problem is not an emotional issue for your therapist. You can achieve similar wisdom by thinking clearly and carefully and examining the problem without jumping to conclusions. The following exercises are designed to help you do this. Remember, the object is cooperation, and both of you are concerned about getting both your needs met.

Richard grins mischievously at me whenever we go to a wedding at which a certain popular ritual is observed, because he feels me squirming in my seat. I get restless and fidgety whenever I see a couple light two candles, representing their individuality, then use their individual candles to light a larger one. I love the symbolism of two individual lights creating a larger, brighter one, but where I have trouble is when the pair then blow out their own candles, and the minister says something like, "Two have now become one."

My reaction to this is extreme discomfort, which is terribly unfair and judgmental, because I have no way of knowing exactly how the couple being married interpret the ceremony. Also, they have every right to have whatever ceremony they wish without my approval.

I mention this only to illustrate what I hope to accomplish in this section. Let's create the greater light, the warmer glow, and then display it proudly along with our individual lights. You don't have to extinguish any part of your God-given, special, individual flame in order to be in love. In fact, as long as you keep your individuality intact, you're capable of uniting and rekindling a larger flame at any moment. Two do *not* become one—they become something *more* than two. How much more is unlimited, and can continue to grow for a lifetime.

You may find it helpful to keep the picture of the three flames in mind while doing the following exercises.

EXERCISES FOR INDIVIDUALS

Because you're working on your own, these exercises are mostly about *listening* and *understanding.* The key to the process is to find out what the essence of your individual lovestyle is, and you probably already have an idea from doing the previous exercises. Having that information, you can then check it out with your partner and begin your synthesis. Actually, you'll find that the longer you've been together, the more synthesis has already occurred. This process is merely to help you encourage synthesis in the areas where you haven't done it naturally, or to correct what you've already done to make it more effective for you.

If you're worried about doing it "all by yourself," relax. You and your partner will wind up doing it together if you follow the guidelines. Your partner won't feel he/she is doing "exercises" unless you express it that way. If your partner finds that he/she *enjoys* the process (don't be too surprised), you can then talk about this book and what you want to accomplish. Otherwise, just allow these techniques to become part of your normal communication, which is where they belong, anyway.

If this is a difficult time in your relationship, or you are very anxious about this, you may want to do some preliminary work to prepare yourself. I recommend affirmations and creative visualization for calming yourself effectively. The books, *I Deserve Love* by Sondra Ray (Celestial Arts, 1976); *Creative Visualization* by Shakti Gawain (Whatever Publishing, 1978); and *A Conscious Person's Guide to Relationships* by Ken Keyes (Loveline, 1975), all contain very helpful ways to create a solid inner base from which to begin communication.

No matter what's happening in your life today, do these exercises with the same gentleness you've done all the prior exercises. Go slowly and easily and you won't frighten yourself or your partner.

Exercise No. 1

Referring back to your book, especially the various exercises about knowing how you are loved and loving, make four lists:

(1) A list of the essential ingredients that *must* exist in your relationship.

(2) A list of those qualities you'd *like*, but don't consider essential.

(3) A list of the things you're *not* willing to have in your relationship.

(4) A list of the qualities you'd *rather not* have, but could live with.

Remember, none of this is cast in stone—it's just a process of evaluating intangibles, and you can change your mind later. You'll learn a lot about yourself just from making the lists. Being clear about your wants is your objective.

After you've made your lists, take some time to arrange them by priority, putting the most important things on each list at the top and moving the least important down to the bottom.

When you've made your lists, you'll probably have a clearer idea of your priorities, which will give you a better chance of communicating effectively. Read them over, make changes if you wish, and save them in your journal.

Exercise No. 2

Now make the same set of lists for your partner. Yes, I know you're only guessing, but you probably know more about your partner than you realize, and we'll find some ways to check your guesses for accuracy.

Once you've imagined the four lists your partner would make, prioritize them, reread them and see if they're appropriate to what you know about your mate. Save these in your journal, too.

Exercise No. 3

With both sets of lists at your disposal, you can begin a subtle process of checking out your guesses. Start with the highest priorities, and when you see those qualities being demonstrated in other relationships—on TV, among friends and relatives—ask your partner how he/she feels about them occurring in your relationship. *Do not* give your own opinion at this time—especially if it differs from the one you believe your partner holds. By sharing your feelings now, you could influence your partner's viewpoint. If you're specifically asked for your evaluation, of course you can speak—but remember, the main focus here is learning, not teaching.

As always in matters of communication, the mood is important. This is not a debate, it's an attempt to learn about your partner. These discussions must be relaxed and easygoing to be effective. If you get no response, or a response that doesn't satisfy you, let it go—and come back to it (gently) later, when the discussion has been forgotten. When the response is informative, reinforce it—let your partner know you're glad to know his/her opinion.

Take a period of time to check out your guesses—weeks or months. After all, this is a lovestyle you're building for a lifetime. Take time to do it carefully.

At any time, if your partner shows interest in this subject, you can (gently) mention this book and the work you've been doing, and invite your partner to share your learning. However, don't insist. Badgering, pushing, cajoling, begging, etc., will only push your partner away. In fact, if you do find your partner moving away, you can assume he/she feels pushed, even if you're not aware of pushing.

Perhaps your partner is interested in your questions and enjoys the discussions, but doesn't want to do a whole series of exercises. OK, in that case you can be more assertive and direct with the questions. Always let your partner know you value his/her opinion. And always make sure your timing for this is right. Avoid becoming boring or a nuisance—that kills enthusiasm.

Another way to check your guesses is to ask relatives. This is not to encourage you to talk with others about your partner in a negative way, or to appear to be "sneaking around." That's not the point. It's the difference between a wife going to her husband's mother and saying, "Harry's such a picky eater—was he always like that?" and then having a discussion of the "trouble with Harry," and the wife going to the mother and saying, "I'm not sure I know what foods Harry likes. What can you tell me?" The first scene leads to everyone feeling uncomfortable and negative. The second can be filled with fond memories and warm thoughts, and both people can feel good about their involvement.

For your own sake, if you're going to check out your ideas with friends and relatives, do it in a kind, loving way, seeking advice and information. You'll feel better about it, and you won't have betrayed your partner, your friends or yourself. Revise your lists according to what you learn.

EXERCISES FOR NEW RELATIONSHIPS

Exercise No. 1

Separately, each of you make four lists:

(1) Relationship aspects I must have to be satisfied.

(2) Aspects that would be nice, but aren't essential.

(3) Things I'd rather not have to deal with.

(4) Aspects I absolutely don't want to face.

Don't share your lists yet. Remember that these lists are not carved in stone; they're just guidelines and can be changed later. Also, they can be about the emotional, physical, mental and material aspects of relationships. For example, if you consider a certain financial status important, now's the time to put it on your list. If you find certain kinds of affection equally vital, they go there, too, along with such intangibles as honesty, mutual respect, etc.

Whether you approve of these conditions or not, they're yours and must be dealt with. You'll probably find it helpful to go back into your book and notice what you came up with in prior exercises, especially, "I feel loved/loving when . . ." All we're doing now is organizing the ideas and concepts of your lovestyle so that they'll be easier to communicate.

Once you've made your lists, rearrange the order of the items according to how important they seem to you now. This could change from day to day, so don't worry about it; it's just another way to help you organize your thoughts. When the lists are done and prioritized, put them away and ponder them a while. You may want to rewrite, scratch out, do over—that's fine, as long as you don't get too anxious about it. This is just a starting point.

When your lists are finalized, begin to share them. First, look for those items that are similar for both of you; next, look for those that seem easy to harmonize; and last, focus on those that feel different or incompatible.

Discuss possible ways you can allow for the differences in your relationship without struggle. Project possibilities into the future, including both the best and worst combinations of your wants and gifts.

Allow this time of projection to be light and fun. What you're doing here is creating a model of your "possible relationship," and also forewarning yourself of pitfalls. Years later, you'll be surprised at how accurate your guesses and fantasies were.

Stan Dale and Val Beauchamp, in *Fantasies Can Set You Free* (Celestial Arts, 1980), describe the power of fantasy:

> The untapped power residing in human fantasy is comparable to the untapped energy in the ocean's tides. Understanding and using the power of fantasy can reshape your outlook, personality, disposition, and ultimately your life. You can rid yourself of emotional handicaps acquired in the past and release the real person who has been afraid to come out.

This is your chance to use that power to begin to shape and blend your unique lovestyles, your disparate wants and needs and the special gifts you have for each other, into a smooth, functioning whole.

This process has particular value for me, because I was so nervous about marrying Richard that I spent a great deal of time contemplating what it might be like. Even though this sounds like "negative" planning, I took a good hard look at who we were, and where that might create a problem.

I wasn't having any problem seeing the "positive" possibilities, I was in love!

Four years later, I find that I was right: we do have problems where I expected us to. The advantage is that nothing has come as a surprise. When a problem arises, it's something I've already considered, at least in a general sense, and I've already taken a look at how to solve it. Of course, there's no way to know the details, or *how* and *when* the problem will arise. Still, having even a vague idea of what the problem is about and how to solve it (even when "how to solve it" was, "Boy, if *that* one comes up, we'd better get to a therapist right away!") has given me a "leg up" and helped me think more clearly.

Think of this as a "fire drill" for future problems and a blueprint for building the relationship you want. Don't forget to have fun!

Don't let nervousness about "self-fulfilling prophecies" hamper your willingness to look at your negative expectations. What we want to do here is uncover these negative expectations and counteract them. Pretending they're not there won't prevent their fulfillment; finding antidotes will.

You already know I'm going to suggest that you write your results down in your book, don't you?

Exercise No. 2

Another angle of approach to this is to look at past relationships.

What was so important you were willing to fight the person you loved about it? This is especially helpful if you have a tendency to discount your own needs as important. They always come up eventually, and if they've been denied, they come up with a fury!

How were you most successful in your past relationships? Were you always the calming influence? Were you a good communicator? A good provider?

Look for past patterns: whatever came up before is likely to happen again to some degree. When you find a pattern you like, consider ways of encouraging that pattern in this relationship. For example, in the case of needs you denied until you "couldn't take it anymore," you can make sure you give them priority now, before they cause an explosion. When you find a pattern you don't want to repeat, consider what might correct it. Discuss how you can help each other with these patterns. One way is to remember who you are when your partner is afraid you're "just like" his/her ex. This will help you resist acting like the ex, despite whatever unconscious encouragement you're getting.

Write down your discoveries. They'll be a very handy reference source later.

Exercise No. 3

Now, make separate lists of your assets: what you bring to the relationship. You've been discussing this, along with wants and worries, for the past two exercises, so you'll have quite a list by this time. Then, make a list of your partner's assets as *you* see them. We're talking about what you believe he/she has to offer, what you hope to gain by being together.

Share your lists. Amplify them with each other's suggestions. If your partner's list contains any assets (yours or his/hers) that you don't understand, be sure to ask for clarification. Knowing exactly what your partner thinks about this will be very helpful in the future.

Record the completed lists in your book.

Exercise No. 4

Now, to help loosen up your thinking, you're going to play a word game. For every item on your lists, come up with the most *positive* synonyms (words with the same meaning) possible. Use a thesaurus, if you like. Rewrite your lists as positive qualities. For the items you don't want, find positive alternatives. For example, if you don't want cheating and infidelity, a positive alternative is that you *do* want faithfulness, honesty and reliable agreements.

We're all so used to thinking in negative terms (somewhere, many of us got the idea it was "more polite" to think negatively about ourselves), we need practice in thinking positively. Revising your lists into positive terms will make it much easier to find ways of synthesizing these relationship qualities.

Write your revised lists in your book. You'll use them in the next session.

EXERCISES FOR LONGTERM RELATIONSHIPS

The longer you've been together, the more synthesis you've already accomplished. Our task here is not really to teach you synthesis, but to make you aware of the synthesis you've already achieved, and to help you smooth out the rough places. You may also find it helpful to read the last section ("New Relationships" exercises), which is about how synthesis is created from scratch.

It's also possible that some of the blending of styles you have achieved has been through sacrificing things important to you. (One of my clients gave up flying kites on the beach because "married women don't do that.") If so, you may have some resentment about this. Don't be overly concerned with your anger. As you correct this situation and reclaim what you've renounced, the bitterness will fade. You only need the anger as long as your needs aren't being valued.

Exercise No. 1

Separately, each of you make a list of what you like and another of what you don't like in your present relationship. After allowing time to work on your lists, share them, either out loud or by exchanging them, and compare.

Discuss your differences and your agreements. Can you see where your individual styles are reflected in your lists? Go back and compare the information you got from the "I feel loved by you when . . . " exercise. Compare the loved/loving information with these lists about what you like. Do they complement each other? In your discussion, also consider what you *don't* have in your relationship—both what you'd like to have and what you're glad you left out. Compare this with other relationships you see around you.

What you're doing here is establishing your basic relationship goals before you begin considering how to achieve them. It's OK if you don't get everything now. You're learning a process you can use over and over again, anytime a change is needed. Put your lists in your book for future reference.

Exercise No. 2

Consider what your fights have been about in the past. What are the main issues, and where do each of you stand on them? This is another indicator about what is not negotiable for you.

Don't worry, this process is about learning to *harmonize* what you can't or won't *compromise*. So take some time and come up with a good list. Be careful to consider what the fights were *really* about: for example, were you fighting about your partner's lateness, or about your own feeling that you weren't cared about?

Are there some issues and events that you know in advance will automatically result in a fight? Are there things you attempt to hide from each other just to avoid fights? What are these "loaded" issues? Make a list of these hidden things separately and privately, if you wish. Again, focus on what the *real* core issues are, not on the details of who did what when and to whom.

You may be a bit sweaty-palmed or nervous after you do this for a while. Don't worry. Remember, we're examining these things so we can solve them.

Now consider the best and smoothest times you've had together. What was it about your styles that harmonized so well at those times? Make a list of those good times.

This list will show you where your styles have synthesized well, and also where you might want to focus understanding and negotiation to create an even better synthesis.

All these lists belong in your book.

Exercise No. 3

Consider the aspects of your relationship that seem to mystify you. Is there anything about your partner's lovestyle that you haven't understood over the years? Is there anything you feel your partner has never understood about yours?

If you've felt critical in the past of what you never understood, now's your chance to ask some questions. Give yourselves a chance to understand each other. This is a learning process, so it's not appropriate to insist on telling your own viewpoint. Put your attention on understanding your partner's explanation, and repeat what your partner says back to him/her in your own words, so you'll both know you understand.

This kind of exploration is the hardest, because you're looking at whatever has baffled you during the time you've been together. Any time you feel overloaded, take a break. Don't let yourselves get discouraged. If you'd like some reassurance, look ahead to the next section of exercises. You'll see that we focus right away on resolving these difficult issues.

Also, if you have trouble here, you can go back and forth between this exercise and the next one (No. 4), which will take you from identifying the issue to "detoxifying" it. This will enable you to perform both actions on one problem at a time, rather than doing all the identifying at once, and then all the detoxifying. Notes in your journal will also be helpful.

Because I'm not there with you, I can't judge your pace and the atmosphere as I would in couple counseling, so you must do these things on your own. Keep the process appropriate for yourselves. If a particular exercise is very difficult for you, put it aside and choose what suits you best at this time.

Exercise No. 4

Now, looking at your lists and all the things you feel strongly about, it's time to adjust your thinking. Look for the *positive* value of each item.

If the issue is dishonesty, look at how more honesty could clear up your confusion. Also, look at the motives behind any dishonesty there has been between you. It was probably an attempt to spare someone's feelings, which is kind, or an attempt to avoid a hassle, which is also understandable. You can now correct the confusion and teach each other what would *really* spare your feelings or avoid a hassle.

In his article, "Trusting and Truthing" (*In Context*, Summer 1985), Stan Dale says: "We are so afraid of hurting others and of being hurt that we do the very thing that is guaranteed to destroy what we cherish."

Even though what we've done hurts, we can acknowledge the caring impulse behind it and make the correction.

Put at least as much energy into this as you did in the last exercise. I believe you get what you focus your energy on, and we want to create positive results here, so don't skimp when you focus energy on changing those negative ideas around.

When you have your list translated into positive aspects,

record it in your book (you may want to throw out the old list and just keep the new one).

SECTION II

BRAINSTORMING/EXPERIMENTING/
CELEBRATING

Congratulations! You got through the roughest part! OK, now onto new thinking and the creative process.

In human relationships, we need to explore what I call "the unthinkable" if we are going to create new possibilities on which to base our behavior. In other words, we have to think about what we don't want to think about —"the enemy." We need to transport ourselves right into the "enemy" camp and examine it thoroughly, walk around the territory, get to know it as a native.

. . . Out of my own personal experience, and from working with many people in a wide variety of situations where communication was blocked, relationships were in conflict, and trust was not present, I have become convinced that whatever the circumstances, the process works.

It is hard to establish and hold to this level of unconditional love in human relationships because we have few models in our daily lives on which to draw. We simply have not been taught to do it. Certainly *my* parents' generation were heir to the belief that parenting involved controlling, correcting and molding the behavior of children. They believed in a model that represented humankind as basically flawed, unable to function independently or

161

without conflict, needing authority and control. If we believe that is how human beings relate to one another, we will be proved right. If, on the other hand, we are willing to entertain other possibilities, to create new models, we will see very different results.

As we dissolve blocked communications through letting go of our belief in the enemy, we are creating a new model. I submit that part of this new model must include the belief that *when we honor diversity, we have no enemies.* (Jane Hughes Gignoux, "Letting Go of the Enemy," *In Context*, Summer 1985.)

The truth is, no one can create change from outside. No matter how much you want to help a beloved person change, you cannot do it as long as you remain the enemy. Since effective change can only be made when someone is motivated to do it for him/herself, the only thing you can do from outside is offer suggestions or advice, and that type of advice is only acceptable from a valued and admired friend, never from an enemy. Advice from a hostile outsider is only refused, never absorbed.

Therefore, to change your relationship, you must be willing to do it as friends. Together, working as a cooperative team, you can solve almost any issue that comes up. Each of you, in that context, can view each other as a friend, a help, a support system.

Within an atmosphere of mutual understanding, mutual help and mutual caring, these processes will help you create profound changes, easily and effortlessly. Whenever you feel yourself resisting, struggling, working too hard or viewing your partner as your "enemy," *stop.* Do whatever you need to do to correct the atmosphere before you proceed. Keep it light and easy, and have fun!

EXERCISES FOR INDIVIDUALS

In these exercises, you'll continue to open the communication between you and your partner. Gentleness, of course, is always a key. The more you let your partner know that you view him/her positively, and the more you can find ways to appreciate and encourage, the faster and easier the doors will open.

Remember, your partner will *not* make changes unless he/she is motivated; that is, unless he/she has a reason to change that's important to him/her. Therefore, it's in your best interest to allow your partner to discover his/her own reasons to change. Making a change yourself is often the simplest way of allowing your partner to discover his/her own motivation to change.

The thing most of us are tempted to do is *persuade* others to "be reasonable—see it my way." Unfortunately, that approach is more likely to arouse resistance in the other person. It only makes the job more difficult. If there is something going on that upsets you, look for the changes *you* can effect that will make the problem your partner's and not yours.

Take yourself out of the problem and give your partner a chance to see it clearly. Amazingly, you'll see your partner become motivated to solve his/her problem without a single word from you. In fact, that's one way to make sure you're not persuading or coercing your partner. Don't use words, simply do what you must to get out of the way of his/her problem, so he/she can see it for what it is. As long as you're upset, frazzled and otherwise involved, the problem appears to be yours.

That process, in tandem with these exercises, will produce amazing results, even if your partner *never* agrees to work on the relationship.

Exercise No. 1

You already have two lists from the prior exercises: your partner's lovestyle priorities and yours. In this step, you begin to change *your* thinking, which is a prerequisite to creating change in your relationship. With copies of your "must-have" lists side by side, begin to visualize the strength of these different values when used harmoniously.

This change in thinking can be difficult at first, especially if you're used to thinking of differences in a relationship as "bad." Actually, it's from your differences that you generate excitement in your relationship. The similarities create security and peace; the differences create excitement and challenge. Relationships last the longest with a balance of both.

Looking at your "must-have" lists, begin to evaluate each strong desire of your own and estimate each of your partner's from a positive point of view. For example, if he/she is more worried than you about cleanliness and tidiness, view this as a quality of being highly organized, rather than being "too picky." Or, if he/she doesn't want to be home at a regular time every night, see that as "spontaneous and unstructured," rather than "irresponsible."

The best example of this process I can think of was a revelation I had with my dear friend and partner, Riley Smith. We have been close for about ten years, and the relationship is very rewarding, although the difference in our tastes, views and opinions is astounding.

The revelation came at a time when we were struggling over our difference in styles, because we were leading workshops together. Riley is very organized, wants an outline, wants to feel well-prepared. I, on the other hand, like to talk "off the cuff" and rely on my inspiration and intuition, bouncing off the people and the immediate events. For a while we struggled over whose way was right. Then, when we switched the focus to how we could *both* be right, suddenly everything fell into place. We began to see how Riley's focus on organization and logical order could be the foundation and structure *within* which I could be free to use my intuitive skills. Immediately we both became more powerful than we had been and found our appropriate team relationship.

I no longer had to worry about any organization at all—Riley would happily handle that. He benefited because I would handle the nonsequiturs and unexpected events of the moment. That division of responsibility worked like a clock. Yet, when either of us leads a workshop alone, we can still handle all the functions. The teamwork merely allows us to focus on our strength.

If one of you likes to socialize, but the other prefers a quiet evening at home, examine those wants as to how they can strengthen each other. Let the "social butterfly" be in charge of parties, and let the "homebody" shine on your quiet evenings together. All relationships have opportunities for both. The social one can help make parties easier for the quiet one, getting him/her settled in a cozy nook with some good conversationalists. On evenings at home, the one who shines there can take care to make home comfortable, inviting and cozy. Each of you will appreciate the other's skill when you benefit from it.

Check out your lists, noticing those qualities that are automatically compatible, and then use your imagination on the differences. Give yourself a chance to get used to this new way of thinking about your differences and seeing them as gifts instead of problems.

Be sure to write your ideas in your book—you'll want to remember them until you have a chance to use them.

Exercise No. 2

Now that you've done Exercise 1, you'll have an idea of how to present your ideas of synthesis to your partner. At this point, don't go too fast. Think about the things that are most important to your partner, and find ways to encourage and appreciate them, in conjunction with your own favorites.

For example, if he/she loves watching sports on TV and you don't, try inviting couples over for a big sports event, and get a game of *Trivial Pursuit* going for the nonenthusiasts in another room. Or have a do-it-yourself gourmet cooking class, and let the sports fans sample the results.

After the party (or other experiment) has been successful is the time to talk to your partner about the synthesis. Simply mention that you thought it would be a good chance for both of you to do what you like most and still be together.

Keep recording your findings and results in your book. You'll find that they're very effective indicators of how you're doing.

At any time, especially if you're gentle and effective, you may find your partner becoming curious about what you've been learning and where the changes came from. That's the time to invite him/her to join you in the exercises for couples. If he/she declines, just answer any questions and let it go for now. Stay with this exercise for a while, until you've had a few successes. Record your successes in your book.

Exercise No. 3

Now it's time for a slightly more direct approach. Again going back to your lists for reference, open a conversation something like this: "I've been thinking, and it seems to me that you want _____ and I want _____. Do you think if we combined them and did _____, it would work?"

You fill in the blanks. Here, it's again important to be gentle; this whole process may try your patience sorely. Don't despair! You'll see the progress; in fact, you've probably seen it already. Remember, with the old way you were stuck completely. Once things have begun to move with this new thinking, both of you will be encouraged, and the movement will become smoother and faster.

Go back and update your lists as you find out more and more about your partner's preferences and yours. Keep a record of what works best, and also of anything that's counter-productive. At best, this can free up your relationship issues to the point that you feel satisfied and can stop all this experimenting. At worst, you'll probably have a very clear picture of where the "stuck places" are, and of where you need help to see better options.

Always hold open the option for counseling. It's difficult for me to imagine my own relationship being as successful as it is without the counseling we've had. When you're emotionally attached to a problem, it's difficult to see it clearly or think effectively about it. The techniques you've learned in this book can help you think more clearly, and clear thinking can enable you to make great changes for the better.

However, we all have emotional times when we can't think clearly, or we don't understand the problem enough to think about it effectively at all. Also, anyone can get tired of doing "all the work." At those times, a good supportive, understanding therapist can be a real necessity. Don't deny yourself the help you deserve when you need it.

Exercise No. 4

Now for what is perhaps the most important technique for success in your relationship. *Celebration!* Pay close attention to your successes, however small or grand they are.

Remember to celebrate yourself and your willingness to enhance your relationship with a pat on the back, lunch with a good friend, a fragrant bubble bath, a day off from work, a new tie or scarf or just a gold star pasted in your book!

Then celebrate every step of the way: the completion of each exercise, each new experiment, each successful response from your partner—celebrate every chance you get!

As you begin to have more and more successes, gently call your partner's attention to them and thank him/her for whatever part he/she played in the success. For a large success, suggest a celebration that satisfies both your celebrational styles.

As you celebrate, notice what your celebration styles are and how you're successfully combining them. Go back to the exercise about holidays and celebrations and use it for reference.

Celebrate, too, with your book. Make a special page for a milestone: use stickers, crayons, cut out magazine pictures, etc., to make that page special. Anytime you feel discouraged, go back and look at your celebrational pages— it can be very encouraging.

As I've said before, I believe you get what you focus on. Focusing on celebration gives you more energy for the successes in your relationship, and more reasons to celebrate! It also ensures that you notice your accomplishments, which gives you more energy to proceed further.

As before, discuss how you can best combine these strong points within your relationship and learn to make the most of them. Celebrate how wonderful you both are, and how lucky you are to have each other for this great adventure. Make giant signs about how wonderful you think you are and put them up all over your house(s).

Be extra detailed when you write these exercises in your book, so you'll have this litany of virtues to revive you whenever you get discouraged or worried. Reminding myself and Richard of how wonderful we are is the best way I know of to move a "stuck" struggle into a successful discussion.

EXERCISES FOR NEW RELATIONSHIPS

Exercise No. 1

Together, look at your lists of important wants from Exercise 1 in the last set of exercises. Pick out the wants that seem most irreconcilable, most opposite. Now consider the list in which you renamed these qualities in a more positive light. Can you see how they could complement or blend better?

Look at your partner's list for those qualities you'd like to learn, or that you can see would benefit you. Remember, the point is to find ways to blend the two in a workable way, *not* to change your wants. You want to see how to enhance them by using the benefits of each.

Begin to use your imaginations to create ways of blending the two "opposites": play with possibilities, silly scenarios, wild fantasies, etc. Let your imaginations run free! For example, if one of you likes outdoor physical activity and the other likes to be comfy indoors, imagine a scene in which one is scuba diving and the other is relaxing on a fancy yacht.

At this point, don't focus on whether your ideas are *possible* or not, don't worry about whether they're sensible or rational. This is called "brainstorming," and the point is to allow your mind to run free, so you'll "loosen up" and come up with ideas you've never had before. Openness to ideas is the important issue.

Give this process at least half an hour; then, in your book, list the most delightful and exciting options, the ones that could really work, any that seem important to you. You have begun the synthesis process.

Exercise No. 2

Now that you have begun thinking synthesis, begin to look around for examples of synthesis in other relationships. Look around at other couples you know, family and friends, and look for synthesis in action in their relationships. Where have they denied their differences? Where have they used synthesis to enhance their individuality? Who has done the best job of synthesis? Look at people in the media and characters in the movies, on TV and in fiction, and find examples.

Write them down and weigh them against your own ideas gleaned from brainstorming. Use these examples to stimulate new ideas for yourselves.

Exercise No. 3

Once you've completed Exercise 2, you're ready to bring some of your plans into actual use. This is an experimentation phase, a chance to try out new ideas. *It's not necessary for everything to work the first time you try it!* The nature of experimentation is trial and error, trial and success. If you experiment with something that doesn't work, keep your sense of humor and use it as an opportunity to learn. Rarely will something be a total disaster. Figure out which parts of it worked, and which didn't.

Remember that none of these experiments is a foregone conclusion—you don't have to do it the same way forever. It's just an experiment. Be willing to experience each other's favorite styles, as well as your own.

Done with gentleness and humor, this exercise can be lots of fun. In order to allow the fun to happen, you need to relax the rules and stay away from "right and wrong," "shoulds" and "oughts." You'll probably discover some new options you didn't think you could ever have.

Like scientists, record the results of your experimentation in your book.

Exercise No. 4

Now, for the present moment set aside a small part of your awareness to observe yourself. Remember, I said observe— not criticize. Look for the places where synthesis is happening in your relationship. Look for the "jargon" that you're both learning to use, the special, shared words and phrases that are only meaningful to you.

Watch for ways in which your individual personality traits are blending smoothly into a "team effort." Look also at couples around you to observe synthesis in action. You can learn from both the good examples and the bad ones. By this time, you have considerable familiarity with each other, and you're beginning to see how you work together.

Any time you find a place where you have "rough spots" and your individual styles don't blend well, look for a way to synthesize them. Go back to some of the earlier exercises, or on to the exercises for Longterm Relationships, next, for more information when you need it.

Celebrate every bit of synthesis you can find, and congratulate yourselves because you care about your relationship, your selves and each other. The more you value your individuality and your partner's, the smoother the process of synthesis will be.

Design your celebrations to be a synthesis of your different styles, too. Go back to the section on holidays and celebrations and use the ideas you discovered there to enrich your celebrations now.

Remember that the more fun you have with this, the better it works.

Record your new designs for celebrating in your book. Learning to celebrate, and remembering to do it, are the most effective techniques for success I know. The more frequent and the more fun your celebrations are, the more successful you'll feel. And the more successful you feel, the more success you'll have.

More than any other single factor, relationship longevity corresponds to the feeling of success experienced by the people in the relationship. Who would want to leave a good thing? As your relationship grows, check out the exercises for Longterm Relationships, especially those regarding celebration.

EXERCISES FOR LONGTERM RELATIONSHIPS

Synthesis is not new to you: as you look around, you'll discover that a great deal of it has already happened during the time you've spent in your relationship. Some of the synthesis will be beneficial and enhancing to each of you and your relationship, and some will feel detrimental and stifling. The task now is to correct what isn't working and to find ways to synthesize the parts that still feel irreconcilable between you.

Exercise No. 1

Spend a few days "researching" synthesis: look around at friends and family members you've known for a while and see how they've adjusted their styles to fit each other or to fit new situations, such as a new baby, retirement, new job, new house or children growing up and moving away.

What do you like about what you observe?

What looks unpleasant or difficult to you?

Do you know anyone who has apparently "given up" most of his/her own personality and taken on his/her mate's?

Who do you see learning to mesh well together, yet keeping their independent selves intact?

How did your parents do it?

Do you want to do it the way they did, or how would you do it differently?

Record your observations and thoughts in your book.

Exercise No. 2

Check out Exercise 2 for New Relationships in this section and have your own "brainstorming session." If you have children living at home, bring them in on it and ask them for suggestions. Small children, especially, brainstorm well, because they haven't developed their internal "censors" yet and are usually more free to be creative.

Use your imaginations to blend your differences: play with possibilities, silly scenarios, wild fantasies, etc. Let your imaginations run free! If you're doing this with children, let them lead. They're automatically experts at imagination!

At this point, don't focus on whether your ideas are *possible* or not, don't worry about whether they're sensible or rational. This is called "brainstorming," and the point is to allow your mind to run free, so you'll "loosen up" and come up with ideas you've never had before. Openness to ideas is the important issue.

Because you have a shared history, you have the added opportunity to brainstorm new solutions for some of your past fiascos. Look for places where you got "stuck" in your differentness and brainstorm new, creative, even silly solutions for those problems. But before you begin to brainstorm one of these old events, agree on which event to choose for your focus.

Keeping these sessions light and fun enhances your chance for success. This is just to practice generating ideas without censure, so don't strive for a resolution yet. It's OK to have magic solutions, angels, wizards or fairy godmothers come in and fix it! It's OK to have solutions that take more money than you have. The purpose is to free up your blocked thinking.

Write the most notable suggestions in your book.

Exercise No. 3

Now bring your suggestions into your everyday life any way you can. Experiment, practice, play with the new ideas.

For example, try having a meal during which everyone gets to choose his/her own entrée—either frozen, take-out or self-prepared (each prepares his/her own)—and you all eat together, at the same time and place. Then play with food combinations during that meal. What does pizza taste like with Chinese food on the side? How does your favorite tuna casserole or meatloaf go with piroshkis from the deli? What about sushi and chocolate pudding? Perhaps a dish your partner loves but you don't tastes better combined with a favorite food of yours.

Begin bringing synthesis into your lives more and more. Focus on the places where you've felt dissatisfied or disappointed and beam the full force of your creativity there. Find ways to honor the individuality you've neglected, or to open yourself to a new experience you've resisted. Experimenting means testing it out. If you don't like it, you don't have to do it again. Keep only what works.

Record your experiments and experiences in your book, focusing especially on the dynamics that were once problems, but for which you've now learned new options.

Exercise No. 4

Celebration! I've written a lot about it in other places in this book, because I believe it's important. I cannot overemphasize the power of celebrating. Celebrate with ritual, with simple congratulations to yourself and each other, with champagne if you drink or with ginger ale or grape juice in fancy glasses if you don't. Celebrate with dinner out, by bragging to friends, by throwing a party!

Celebration is the recognition of your caring and energy. It focuses your attention on your success, thereby creating more success. It generates enthusiasm and hope. With celebration, you're encouraged to do more and do it better. It accomplishes everything you may have been attempting to accomplish with nagging, blaming, pressuring or criticizing and does it with love and joy.

Record your successful celebrations, your new ideas for celebration that you haven't yet tried, and enjoy yourselves!

SECTION III

REVIEW AND CLARIFY

You have essentially learned the process of synthesis by this time. As you become more familiar with it and adept at it, you can make it a natural, normal part of your relationship.

The final aspect of the synthesizing process is much like insurance. Because there's so much confusion in our society about cooperation and intimacy, and because we all have a tendency to assume that everyone else thinks the same way we do, we need a way of knowing when we're communicating effectively.

It's surprisingly easy to reach an agreement, and then find out later that each party understood the agreement differently. Finding that out usually involves an unpleasant surprise or an awkward readjustment in thinking. Therefore, it's well worth providing some "insurance" for yourselves through review and clarification.

EXERCISES FOR INDIVIDUALS

By this time, you may find that you and your mate are cooperating better and talking more easily about your relationship, and you may no longer feel that you're doing this alone. If so, go on to the sections for people reading this together. If not, don't worry, there's still a lot you can accomplish in the relationship. The main difference is that you'll be the one taking the communication initiative most of the time.

There are many successful relationships in which one partner takes on more of the responsibility for "monitoring" the relationship, and the other takes more responsibility somewhere else, such as financially or with the children. This is simply a type of lifestyle, and it can easily work well for you. Please don't assume that the two of you are doing it "wrong" because you're the only one reading this.

Having chosen this area as your responsibility, you can still invite and encourage your partner's participation.

Exercise No. 1

Once some of your previous experiments have been successful, arrange a time for discussion with your partner. Making a "date" is a lovely way to do this. This is the time to bring your partner up to date on your discoveries.

During your discussion, "confess" what you've been doing (if you haven't already). Confession works best when the experiments have gone well. Check out your partner's opinion on how things are going, making sure he/she sees it as an improvement. If he/she doesn't, stop there and ask for his/her evaluation of how it *has* been going. Place yourself in a listening/learning mode.

If you get agreement that things are going well, as you probably will, then proceed to discuss what you've discovered as a result of your experimentation. Frequently ask for your partner's opinions, agreement or disagreement. The point of this discussion is to begin to make some decisions about which processes work well for you, and which do not: some generalizations, based on your experiments, about how you can synthesize some of your more difficult differences.

This discussion can cover several sessions. It's better to keep it light and easy than to try and accomplish everything in an atmosphere of pressure. There's also a benefit in creating a habit of pleasant, frequent discussions about how you're doing together. If your partner has been avoiding such discussions because he/she expects them to be painful, this will correct that expectation.

Make notes to yourself in your book. You may choose to share the book with your partner now, but again, be gentle. Don't give him/her the feeling that it's the prosecutor's evidence. Find a way to introduce it as a labor of love, a part of yourself that you'd like to shre.

Exercise No. 2

Once you've established this habit of conversation about the well-being of your relationship (I call these "state-of-the-union" discussions), merely keep it going. Focus on mutual understanding, so that you both know what your agreements are once they've been made. "As I understand it, we've agreed that at our next party, you will _____ and I will _____. Is that the way you understand it?" A question such as this can be very effective.

Record your agreements in your book, show your partner your entries in the book often and encourage him/her to add to them. By this time, the quality of your communication will have improved significantly. And anytime you find a problem you can't solve quickly and easily, seek help.

EXERCISES FOR NEW RELATIONSHIPS

Having established the pattern of working together on your synthesis from early in the relationship, you now have a distinct advantage. The only thing actually left for you to do now is to confirm and clarify your agreements, making sure you both understand them in the same way.

Exercise No. 1

After you've experimented for a while with the earlier exercises, begin to draw some implications you can apply to your relationship in a generalized way. Set a time and place and make a date to discuss this. The object is to find some solutions that work in general for you in the "stuck" places.

Once you've gotten this started, draw up an "emergency procedure" notice which you can either post or keep handy somewhere. This notice is like the ones in public buildings that read, "In Case of Fire," or, "Earthquake," and tell you what to do.

Based on your observations and discoveries about yourselves and each other, find from five to ten basic ways to avert "disasters" in your relationship and list them.

For example, you may say, "If Mabel is crying, just hold her and don't offer advice until she asks." Or, "If Fred is angry, just give him room until he calms down. Then offer help or understanding." Or, "When we have trouble at a party, a quiet 'may I have a word with you?' is the signal for us to separate from the others and resolve it temporarily, until we have time to fully discuss it later."

As in other examples, only you can know exactly what your

problems are likely to be and what the solutions are. Writing this notice is effective because, exactly like the notices in public buildings, it'll give you something to do and thereby avert panic. Having a specific instruction to follow will help you regain your composure. It'll also let your partner know you want to solve the problem, and that you're doing what you can to do so.

Please keep the solutions *possible*. Keep them easy and general enough so that you'll be able to use them in most situations that could arise. You won't be able to foresee everything, unless you're more psychic than I am, but forestalling even some of the problems can be very helpful.

Record your emergency procedures in your book as well as on the sign.

Exercise No. 2

The only remaining thing is to remember to review your "state of the union" periodically. I recommend you do this weekly at the beginning, until it becomes a habit. Make the meetings light and pleasant—not a heavy obligation. After a while, you'll find you miss them if they don't happen.

The only time Richard and I do this ritualistically anymore is just prior to our anniversary, when we review our status and formally renew our contract. Then we celebrate on the anniversary date. At other times, this review has become so automatic, it just happens, easily and naturally. Either of us has the right to request a review anytime we feel the need. This smooth flow of events has come about because we did review our status regularly for the first several months we were together.

During your review, remember to focus on *understanding* your partner, rather than on telling your story. There's plenty of opportunity for both of you to be heard. Whatever agreements you reach, make sure you both understand them.

EXERCISES FOR LONGTERM RELATIONSHIPS

At this point, you've learned some new skills, and more important, a new attitude toward your different styles. Because of your experimentation, you're beginning to realize that differences can be an advantage, rather than a problem.

The more you practice synthesis, and the more you view your relationship from this viewpoint, the better it gets. The goal is not to make you "clones" or exact copies of each other, but to enhance your individuality and allow it to enhance your relationship. The more color you skillfully blend into your picture the more you'll like to look at it.

Remember to keep the celebrations frequent and fun—to keep your energy moving.

This last section is brief and includes a way to review and clarify your progress and agreements.

Exercise No. 1

Set aside some time for a "state-of-the-union" discussion. Make it a quite time alone together, or a "date," as long as it feels good to both of you. The idea is to spend some time contrasting how you were with how you are now. Focus on how this time of learning and experimentation has affected each of you and your relationship. Your goal is to listen to and understand each other. Find out what each of you has learned, and what has changed for you.

Review your "experiments" and begin to draw some conclusions about what works for the two of you when you're struggling. Also include those solutions you had before you started this project. Keep the solutions as simple and general as you can, so they'll be useful in most circumstances.

Then, as in Exercise 1 for New Relationships, draw up an "In Case of Emergency" poster. In it, include all the things you know from experience will work for you (review the instructions in Exercise 1 for New Relationships). You have your experience to draw on, as well as this new information.

This is the time for both of you to ask for the particular help you need in an emotional emergency. Remember to be sure you can actually do what your partner requests (you can leave room for bad days or mistakes, too). If it seems impossible to you, work with it a while to see if you can adjust it to fit. Remember, you're giving yourself a chance to avoid large hassles, so stretching a little may be worth it. If you find the Time-Out technique, as explained earlier, useful—put it on your poster.

When you get your emergency measures worked out, write up a poster for display or keeping handy, and also write them in your book.

Exercise No. 2

Review Exercise 2 for New Relationships. Set up a format for regular "state-of-the-union" discussions, until they become a natural part of your lives.

You may want to make some of these regular discussions "state-of-the-*family*" discussions and include the children or other members of your household. The easier it is for everyone to express their opinions and feelings to the group, the less often those feelings and opinions need to erupt explosively, or in complaining and nagging tones.

The key issue is that you understand each other, and that you're certain both (or all) of you understand any agreements you make. At best, these discussions will eliminate fighting and frustration, and at worst, they can warn you in advance of the need to seek outside help. No matter what, your relationship will benefit from them.

This is a good time to update your book on a regular basis. One of the best parts of your meetings can be writing family milestones: birthdays, weddings, anniversaries, passings, births, graduations, etc., in a ceremonious and celebrational way. You can also make the book a regular part of any family ritual. Sometimes recording it in the book is all you need to make it an "official" celebration.

SECTION IV

THE TOYBOX

One of my clients gave me this concept after his first session. He called me to tell me how excited he was and how well he was doing. At the end of our first session, I handed him a small pile of articles, some of which I'd written myself, and others which I'd gotten from magazines or excerpted from books (some are quoted in this book).

I do this with all my clients, while explaining to them that they are bombarded daily with lots of "toxic" information, both from their own inner confusion and from friends, relatives, lovers and the mass media. These articles (chosen from my selection of many) are selected specifically for each client according to the problems we've discussed that day. They're to be used as a resource, whenever the client feels overwhelmed.

The young man who called me said, "Those articles are like a toybox! Whenever I have a few minutes, I leaf through the stack and select one to read. It always has a good idea I can play with!"

Using his metaphor, I suggest you create your own "toybox" of books, cartoons, cassette tapes, copies of articles from magazines, poetry, pictures, signs, letters or papers you may have written. Keep these resources in a handy place: a good reading spot at home, in your bedside table, in your desk at work. Choose items which can help calm you down when you're upset, make you smile or laugh when things get too heavy, remind you what's *really* important to you. Remember that help is always available to you, and you'll soon begin to think clearly again.

You'll recognize items suitable for your toybox when you see them. Even videotapes of good movies (workshops, too) can help. Be sure there are some short, easy-to-find things available, as well as longer ones. Mark special passages in books with humorous or beautiful bookmarks, or copy them out.

Once you've accumulated a collection for your toybox, you'll find it a very effective resource, especially for those times (the middle of the night, for example) when your support system of friends and relatives is unavailable, or when they're not helpful.

This resource of reading and visual material is one of the most effective self-help tools I have, and I use it often. Sometimes it provides support, sometimes just new ideas or a pleasant pastime. It has never failed to see me through a panic, to help me calm down enough to think through my problem. Once you decide to create a toybox of your own, you'll find that the contents almost seem to suggest themselves. You may even decide to include a teddy bear for comfort in times of need!

SECTION V

THE YARDSTICK: AN EVALUATION PROCESS

It surprises me how easily I can forget how "it used to be" and believe that I haven't made any progress at all. Many of my clients exhibit the same tendency, and it's one way to feel discouraged and ineffective. When caught in this "hopeless" feeling, it's very helpful to be able to look back into your own history and see how far you've come.

Scott, a client who made great changes in his life, said to me one day: "You know, I thought I was having a bad day today, until I realized that a year ago, this would have been one of my *better* days!"

No matter how well you're doing, today may not be a great day, especially when evaluated against the best days you've ever had. However, if you'll see your life as a yardstick and look back a distance along it, you'll see that the overall quality of your life and relationships has improved greatly.

If you compare others' lives to your own, you may also feel discouraged. That's because you know your life from the *inside*, but you only know theirs from the *outside*. Comparing your life today to your life before gives you a much more accurate picture of your accomplishment.

Another way to discourage yourself is to evaluate yourself on the basis of *someone else's values*. Perhaps you're making less money now than you did, but now you're working in a profession that contributes to humankind, instead of merely making money. Or perhaps you spend less time with your partner than you did before, but now you're really enjoying the time you do have together.

Be clear what your personal yardstick for measuring success is, and measure *by those criteria*, not by your momentary frustration or someone else's criticism.

Here are some ideas to help you create your personal yardstick:

Exercise No. 1

Quickly, without thinking much about it, evaluate this list, putting the items in order of importance to you:

money
laughter
family
clothes
car
world peace
personal effectiveness
pets
romance
career success

    health
    your surroundings
    environmental issues
    human suffering
    religion/spirituality
    fun
    national defense.

Now take a look at your results. This is a deliberately tough list, because we're all faced with these choices (and many more) constantly. There are personal, political, emotional and financial choices we must make every day. If there are some options you'd like to include that aren't on my list, add them in the appropriate order.

I believe that the choices we make, what's most important to us, have less significance than the fact that we each *make a choice!*

Your priorities will change as your life goes on. For example, a young parent must make money a high priority, whereas an older retiree may have the leisure and security to be able to devote lots of time and energy to social, spiritual and/or political causes.

A couple newly in love must focus a lot of energy on their relationship, to the exclusion of other things, because they are building a foundation and support system for all their later priorities.

When I first began to develop my social consciousness, I became overwhelmed by all the problems I saw in America and the world. There was no way I could fix it all! What finally got me energized and encouraged enough to begin was the thought that I could do *one* thing. All I had to do was choose, and if *everyone* chose one priority, together we could fix it all. I've since realized that the same "one-step-at-a-time" approach works in my daily life, too. With chores, business responsibilities, my own personal growth and the requirements of my relationship, frequently life can become overwhelming. But if I restrict my focus to one issue at a time, I find I can be wonderfully effective and gets lots done.

Lewis Anthony Russo, a teacher of Richard's and mine, says, "If you want to get ahead in the world, trust God and do the dishes." By that he means do what you know to do right now, and let the rest take care of itself.

There's no need to feel uncomfortable about your choices. Making choices is the first step toward effectiveness. By making them, you'll create your own yardstick for evaluating your success in each area. In your relationship and in the rest of your life, check in with your yardstick frequently, and you'll see yourself gaining on your goals.

Make a special page in your book for your yardstick and update it periodically.

Exercise No. 2

Have a "remember when?" session with old friends and/or family periodically. Frequently I ask a friend I've known for twenty years to tell me what differences she sees in me since we first met. It's an encouraging reminder of how far I've come. Devote an evening or afternoon to telling each other, "You've come a long way, friend." You'll be surprised how energizing and encouraging it is. Make notes in your book about milestones you've passed and look at them periodically.

Exercise No. 3

At the risk of being redundant, I'll remind you once again to *celebrate!* It's so easy for most of us to emphasize the defeats, the frustrations, the problems, while ignoring all the successes, big and small. Remember, you get what you focus on, so whatever's happening, focus on any successes you can find. Write them in your book, talk about them and celebrate them over and over.

EXPERIENCES

INTRODUCTION

In my workshops, lectures and private counseling, I refer to myself as a "specialist in alternative and creative relationships." I use the word "alternative" only because it's recognized by many of the people I wish to reach. "Creative" is really the word I prefer.

Up to this point in the book, you've learned some theories and techniques about creating relationships that conform to the special and unique needs of the individuals involved. My purpose in this section is to present a sampler of "creative relationships"—some "traditional" and some "alternative."

Actually, I believe the truth is that "traditional" is something we feel we must pretend to conform to, because we can't actually live up to it. In fact, I've never discovered any definition of "traditional relationship" that was acceptable to even a moderate-sized sampling of people. Use monogamy as a definition and people quickly point out the "double standard" and "cheating" that has traditionally happened for centuries.

In the Long Beach *Press-Telegram*, Daniel Winkel says:

Certainly marriage in 1986 is far different from what it was a few generations ago. The rose-colored dreams of a cottage on the corner and eternal wedded bliss have been tempered by economic realty and the changing roles of men and women. Marriage is no longer an expectation, but a choice. And no easy choice at that.

Things we know about marriage and related events: The marriage rate in America is down slightly to 10.2 marriages per 1,000 people in October 1985 from 10.5 in October 1984, according to provisional Census Bureau reports.

The number of divorces is up slightly—from 4.9 per 1,000 people in October 1984 to 5.0 in October 1985, according to provisional Census Bureau statistics.

The median age of first marriage has climbed to a record level for women (23.3 years), while it is nearing a record for men (25.5) years.

The number of unmarried couples living together in America has declined, from 1,988,000 in 1984 to 1,938,000 in 1985, according to a Census Bureau report.

The proportion of people between 25 and 35 who have never married has approximately doubled since 1970, according to the Census Bureau.

Nine out of every 10 women still want to get married, according to the 1985 American Women's Opinion Poll. But 63 percent of the women surveyed want to combine a career with marriage and families, up from 52 percent in 1974.

One more thought-provoking finding: According to the American Women's Opinion Poll of 3,000 women and 1,000 men, 57 percent of all women and half of all men say the best marriage is one in which both the husband and wife work and share household chores and child-rearing responsibilities. Only 46 percent of the women and 44 percent of the men polled in a similar 1974 survey felt that way. (Daniel Winkel, Long Beach *Press-Telegram*, February 16, 1986.)

In the September 1, 1986 issue of *Newsweek*, an article called "Three's a Crowd" contained the following information:

... more and more couples are painting a new kind of American family portrait—one with just two faces, the husband's and the wife's.

The percentage of couples without children has doubled in the last few decades. In 1960 only about 13 percent of married women between 25 and 29 were childless; last year 29 percent were. In the past, motherhood was virtually the only option for married women. That is no longer the case. Today 1 out of 4 ever-married women between the ages of 25 and 34 has never had a child—a total of nearly 3.3 million women—compared to 1 out of 10 women in 1960....

Is it possible to live happily ever after without children? That's like coming out against fireworks on the Fourth of July. But there have always been couples willing to defy tradition, and many have never regretted it ... Some studies have indicated that not having children—if that is what both the husband and the wife want—helps a marriage. In a recent survey, UCLA researcher Bonnie Burman found that couples who decided not to have children rated higher on a marital-happiness scale than couples who chose parenthood....

Many demographers forecast that as many as 20 percent of women now in their early to mid-30's—the first generation of women to have control over their fertility since their teenage years—may never have children, compared with an average childlessness rate of 5 to 10 percent for most of this century. Those numbers will be even higher for women with high-powered careers, the experts say. Harvard economist David E. Bloom, who released a new study of the relationship between women working and childlessness last week in Chicago at the Joint Statistical Meetings, a gathering of professional statisticians, has estimated that 30 percent of all women managers will remain childless . . . Families with two working parents struggle to fit into a work environment geared to the traditional family of the 1950s in which the husband was the breadwinner and the wife the homemaker—*a family structure that now accounts for only about 10 percent of all American households* [italics mine] . . . Finally, there is the example of the current generation of women who are trying to find new ways to maintain the difficult balance between jobs and children. They are, in effect, the shock troops in the re-evolution in women's roles. "They are discovering what works and what doesn't work," says Bloom.

Much has appeared recently in the media regarding the "New Male," the "New Woman," the "New Male-Female Relationship," etc. The March 31, 1986 issue of *Newsweek* had a whole "Lifestyle" section devoted to the difficulties of both sexes in juggling jobs and children—and the creative solutions families are finding. An article on the "New Feminism," included in that section, stated:

By now a generation of women have experienced the stresses and conflicts that inevitably accompany a demanding career. "With liberation comes anxiety, dread, the meaninglessness of choice," says Rutgers University political scientist Benjamin Barber. "This is something that men have always had to deal with." Meeting on this common ground, men and women may finally be able to open up the sort of dialogue necessary for solving problems that ultimately are human, not gender-based. ("Feminism's Identity Crisis")

In an article called, "Are You Sexually Normal?," Marty Klein says:

Worrying about whether your sex life is normal is normal. Sex is a private, hidden activity. Few of us have ever watched another couple making love; it's an unusual person who has seen even five other couples so engaged. Contrast this relative ignorance to the countless experiences you've had watching strangers grocery shopping, noting the contents of their carts, evaluating their health (and judging the behavior of their kids). Add that to the many thousands of people you've watched eat in your life. You know how you stack up to your neighbors in the kitchen. When it comes to the bedroom, however, it's all pretty secretive.

Our culture actually discourages meaningful conversation about such things, so most of us guess about the sex lives of "normal people"—almost always overestimating others' passion, frequency and satisfaction.

Our fantasies about others make it easy to feel inadequate, and media images of sexuality exacerbate the

problem. Although a wide variety of tastes in food, clothing, sports and other elements of life is culturally acceptable, only a narrow range of sexual preferences is
considered normal. . . It's no wonder that most of us—
who don't exactly fit the mold—wonder whether we're
normal. (*New Age Journal*, September 1985.)

The Second Stage, by Betty Friedan, (Summit Books, 1981),
a book about current developments in the "Feminist Movement," makes the following statement:

Men's and women's needs are now converging. There
are conscious choices now, for men as well as women—to
set up their lives in such a way as to achieve a more
equitable balance between success in work and gratification in personal life. And here is the missing link, the
power that was missing when women tried to solve these
problems by taking it all on themselves as superwomen,
the power women did not and will not have, to change
the structure of jobs, by and for themselves alone. But
if young men now need and want self-fulfillment beyond
their jobs and the life-grounding women have always had
in the family—as much as women now need and want
some voice and active power in the world—there will be
a new, and sufficient, *combined* force for the second
stage of feminism.

This is the other half of the struggle that began with the
women's movement for equality—men's liberation. Men,
it seems, are now seeking new life patterns as much as
women.

With all this going on, whatever your lovestyle and lifestyle,
you're most likely experiencing some confusion.

Use heterosexual as your definition of "normal" and the gay community points out, accurately, that homosexual relationships have been common throughout history, as in this quote from *Changing Men* magazine:

> As gay men, we have had to invent ourselves, outside of approved norms for how to be men. Our stories have a common theme of self-creation. I'm not saying that there's not conformity among gay men; I'm saying that there is enormous diversity and experimentation with ways of being men. Since there were no role models, since our families often ignored or even disowned our gayness, since we uprooted ourselves from our pasts to seek each other in urban centers, we were free to find and define ourselves from within. . . .

> Men: think back to a male friend from your pre-adolescent days, a buddy, a playmate who felt close. For almost one man out of three, this male bonding included sexplay (Kinsey, et al., *Sexual Behavior in the Human Male*).

> For others, it was an emotional closeness, a Tom Sawyer-Huck Finn partnership in adventure, a secret club, a gang. In a culture which would prefer to ignore the homosexual potential of its children, such a period is comfortably dismissed as child's play.

> Other cultures are not so denying. In Papua, New Guinea, boys are initiated into manhood by ritualized sexual activity with older men. In ancient Greece gay love was refined and noble. In practically every culture, homosexuality exists.

> Yet our culture conspires to disguise that legacy, sometimes unwittingly. I remember well my sense of betrayal

when I learned that the standard editions of Plato system-atically distort homosexuality, making overtly sexual pas-sages into sublimated scenes more palatable to Victorian morality.

So gay culture lies buried under multiple layers of moral judgment. The painstaking task of reclaiming our culture is a large part of the current gay renaissance. ("The Gay Side of Manhood," Gordon Murray, excerpted in *The Utne Reader*, April/May 1986.)

There are also many variations of age, race, religion, roles (breadwinner/housewife, etc.) and so on. So the words "traditional" and "normal" give me trouble. Hence my problem with "alternative"—alternative to what? There must be a standard or norm in order to have an alternative.

This dilemma is solved by the word "creative." When rela-tionship styles are viewed as creative, then each is unique and special in itself, different from all others, though they may have aspects in common. I believe that all relationships are creative, whether by design or accident. We must make them up as we go along, on the spot—because that's how life is. A relationship, like a life, is shaped partly by response to environment and events, partly by design, partly by ac-cident, perhaps even partly by mistake. We take what has happened, handle it however we can, and when we look back on it, we see the history we call "my life" or "our relationship."

The more information we have about how relationships (or our lives) work, and how to handle them, the more sense of creative control we have. Still, with or without this con-scious choice, we create our relationships, step by step, day by day, as we live them.

Because I perceive a need in this area, my specialty is "training in the art of conscious intimacy" and "creative relationships." Many of the skills involved in "conscious intimacy" turn out to be equally useful in general "conscious living," because that's how human skills are—adaptable and transferable. Once we've mastered a skill in one area, it's frequently possible to extrapolate and use it elsewhere.

Living your relationship according to the guidelines of *Lovestyles* maximizes your creative control over your relationship. Your relationship *is* different from all others, because *you* are different. Being informed merely makes you more able to understand and shape those differences.

Whatever your personal needs and preferences are, the information in the first two parts of this book can help you create a relationship that complements and enhances both your lifestyle and your lovestyle.

Part III has a slightly different purpose. The following is a sampler of actual relationships, described by the people involved. In reading these personal accounts, you can see how innovative, individual and creative relationships can be— while still being successful.

I have an interesting and unusual variety of lifestyle experiences upon which to draw. This is not to suggest that I advocate such experimental living for you. My purpose is not to outrage, confuse or upset you, but to help each of you see that there are *many* successful ways of living and loving.

Please view these examples as options, like the food on the shelves in a store. You're not going to like every choice available: some are almost right, but need to be seasoned to your taste; some may make you break out in hives! Just as in a grocery store, the point is for *you* to choose exactly what's right for *you* from the great variety available.

What I advocate is achieving personal satisfaction and happiness for yourself and your beloved; and I believe that different people need to accomplish this in different ways.

I hope to invite you to think creatively about your own lifestyle and how it can better harmonize with your lovestyle, and the lovestyles of your family members.

Many of the options presented here may be different or unusual or even shocking to you, and you may be tempted to give them more emphasis. Please keep in mind that I personally view *each* livestyle as valid and having the potential for providing satisfaction and a healthy environment for the persons involved.

Of the many options included here that occur among persons I know well, all those involved are consenting and generally quite happy and healthy—even though they have occasional problems. My point is that these are *workable* options and only a tiny sample of the vast variety of relationships individuals have developed to meet their needs.

If you haven't been aware of options like these before, it's because *we don't talk about whatever we're doing that is "different," lest we be censured for it.* However, these choices are being made often, in all areas of the country, in all walks of life.

I hope those of you who recognize an option you may have dreamed about but felt was "wrong" will experience some validation and relief as you realize that what you desire *can* work and that you *can* find others who believe as you do.

Chapter One

LIFESTYLES

Let's begin with the definition of the term "lifestyle." In the first part of this book, I explored style and its origins. It's your unique mode expression of yourself and your feelings, learned and acquired throughout your life.

Life, as I use it here, is actually personal history. What has gone on from birth until now, or some portion of that, is what you usually refer to when you say "my life."

So, your lifestyle becomes the unique expression of your history. I like that definition, because it honors the *entire* lifetime. Today, we often use the term "lifestyle" (as in *Lifestyles of the Rich and Famous*) to mean the possessions and activities of someone at the present time. This often leads to invalidating the *past* experience which has contributed to our present wisdom. What we do and don't do today, and how we feel about it, is intimately connected to our history.

What's the difference between lifestyle and lovestyle? Simply that your *lovestyle* is the expression of your feelings. Your *lifestyle* is the expression of your entire self. Lifestyle is your work, your play, your physical surroundings, your relationships—the context within which you live your life.

Your lovestyle, hopefully, fits into your lifestyle. Neither is entirely controllable, yet both can be highly elective, especially when you approach them consciously and knowledgeably.

CHAPTER TWO

THE VARIETY OF LIFESTYLES AND SOME PROBLEMS WITH THEM

THERE ARE MANY CREATIVE OPTIONS for lifestyles. I'll begin with some from my own experience.

I prefer the idea that my lifestyle is a record of the entire history of my self-expression, through all its many manifestations, culminating in my life as it is today.

Because I tend to be an explorer and experimenter, especially in matters of personal expression, my lifestyle has included many options. (For example, my workstyle has been as creative and experimental as my lovestyle.) I disown none of them, although several were mistakes I had to correct. All my history was essential for me to arrive at where I am today, and I value all of it.

Also, this varied and unusual experience has given me a unique understanding of how different relationship styles are suitable at different times, or with different people.

I have lived:

> in a seven-year, heterosexual, monogamous marriage (until the last year, when I "cheated")

alone and single

in sexually open dating arrangements

with a female roommate (here "roommate" means a nonsexual, living-together relationship)

with a gay male roommate

with a heterosexual male roommate

with six other roommates and a (male) lover (a total of seven adults and two children, including a married couple, two single parents my lover and me)

an ongoing, four-year affair (beginning at age sixteen) with a much older man

and successfully married to a bisexual man (a sexually open relationship and my present one).

I have tried monogamy, celibacy, frequent dating, one-night stands, sexual threesomes, "swing clubs" and homosexual encounters.

Most of these experiences have been enjoyable, and all of them were educational. I don't necessarily recommend such experimentation to you. By preference, I have been experimental in relationships, not because I thought I should, but because of my curiosity. Relationship counseling is the perfect endeavor for me, because it's where my interest naturally lies. My "research" was a natural outgrowth of my curiosity and of my search for a comfortable lifestyle for myself.

As a licensed marriage and family counselor, I have worked with:

"traditional" monogamous heterosexual relationships

longterm gay and lesbian relationships and marriages

single people of both sexes

"living-together" relationships

married and unmarried couples who practice "swinging"

open sexual relationships of all kinds, honest or not

couples living together nonsexually

bisexual relationships (both in which the spouse knows and in which he/she doesn't)

committed relationships with more than two persons

relationships with "reversed" roles (househusbands, wage-earner wives)

post-divorce relationships in which the couple live apart, yet renew their sexual/emotional connection successfully

premarital couples.

So you can see that my variety of experience is useful in knowing how to work with these clients.

There have also been many clients who have had relationship catastrophes:

incest survivors of both sexes

violence survivors of both sexes

children, abused emotionally, physically and sexually

adult children of alcoholics

alcoholics and co-alcoholics (nondrinking family members involved in the disease)

divorced persons

persons with shattered self-esteem

persons with eating disorders.

Relationships are about people; and dealing with the problems in relationships means dealing with the problems of people. Lifestyles can get into grave difficulty, especially because we try so hard to pretend that there is a "right" way to manage them.

Consider "Jim," a father convicted of incest with his daughter, who explains his dilemma: "I started out wanting to help her to avoid being as sexually repressed as her mother and myself—just answering her questions honestly. As it got more and more out of control, I knew it was wrong, but I was afraid to ask anyone about it, until I finally had to turn myself in.

"After seeing what my child had to go through in the courts, I'm not sure I did the right thing. Where can I get help, instead of punishment?"

We seem to find it easier to identify a villain, a "wrong" person, than to focus on the problem and what might work to fix it.

Socially, we're beginning to deal with the results of our "right and wrong" attitudes and discovering the incest, abuse and confusion that has been going on for generations on a huge scale. As we begin to re-evaluate our ideas about right and wrong in relationships, I hope exploring these options can lead to *healthy* self-expression between people who don't feel pressured, condemned, abused or overpowered in their search for love.

CHAPTER THREE

THE ETIQUETTE OF ALTERNATIVE RELATIONSHIPS

THIS IDEA BEGAN AS A RUNNING joke between Richard and me as we ran into many awkward moments sorting out life- and lovestyles with other people. We often said, "Where is Miss Manners (we're great fans of Judith Martin, otherwise known as Miss Manners), now that we need her? What would she say to do now?"

Social conventions make social intercourse much easier. When you know the proper etiquette, you can approach a gathering of strangers with self-confidence. Whenever I encounter a new group of people, I'm always "on my best behavior" until I've observed the group enough to know what *their* accepted standard of behavior is. Then I can relax and join in. This works because I haven't impressed them unfavorably before learning the rules.

Although I may dress very casually with family and friends, I'm always dressed conservatively and correctly for public appearances, because I know my first impression is important.

In alternative relationships, you lose that reassurance of "acceptable standards of behavior." In a society where it's not the "standard" to be gay, how do you discover who else has the same proclivity? If a couple is looking for a third party for sexual play, how do they find out who's a candidate? How does a "swinger" identify another swinger without offending those who aren't? How does a single man approach a woman in this "Age of Liberation"? How does a woman approach a man?

Actually, being as clever as we are, people have evolved some standards to do these things. In the gay community especially, intricate and clever signals of dress and behavior have been worked out to send accurate information about preferences, sexual and otherwise. However, these standards can vary widely from state to state, or from community to community, so the uninformed newcomer has a problem.

Does it surprise you to hear "Joan" say: "I'm attracted to this wonderful woman in my office. We have lunch a lot, and I know she likes me, but how do I find out if she's gay?" Her concern is not to embarrass herself or the other woman, and not to harm a pleasant friendship by upsetting her new friend. Women, more often than men, seem to value friendship over the possibility of sexual contact, if they think they have to make a choice.

I can make a few suggestions about the "etiquette" of such situations—and I hope others will follow and codify more suggestions, so that we can be at ease as our options grow.

Miss Manners will have a lot to forgive me for here, but I'm confident a woman of her grace and poise can manage it.

IN DATING:

(1) BE PATIENT. Generally, if you're interested in an on-going relationship, it's worth waiting awhile and letting things develop to the point that intimate information can be exchanged. Getting anxious and pushing for quick results is more likely to result in a problem.

(2) BE A GOOD LISTENER. Often, the other person will give you valuable clues about preference in ordinary conversation, dropping enlightening "hints" about his/her awareness or ignorance of the desired subject.

(3) WHEN APPROPRIATE, MAKE A DISCLOSURE ABOUT YOURSELF. Once you've developed a basic friendship, you can share something about yourself and your preference. The other person's response will usually be to ignore it, if it's a problem; share his/her own preference if it's similar; or ask interested questions, if he/she wants to know more but doesn't share the preference.

(4) IF (3) IS INCONCLUSIVE, EXPOSE YOUR FRIEND TO A RELATED (GENTLE) ATMOSPHERE. For example, if you're gay, take your friend to a "gay" restaurant for lunch (a nice one) and notice the reaction. Richard and I often show new friends the tape of our appearance on the *Phil Donahue Show,* on which the topic was "Gay Marriages." It's a very clear statement of our attitudes, yet, because it's "out there" on the TV screen, it's not threatening. It usually opens up the conversation.

(5) TAKE A HINT. Anytime you make a suggestion (or maybe even before you get to it), make it easy for the other person to say no. Take silence, reluctance and "maybe" all to mean no. If you're wrong, and the other person meant

yes, he/she will let you know: as soon as you back off, he/she will want to know why. Being easily discouraged in this area is the best way I know to avoid being "the bad guy" later. Have enough respect for yourself and the other person to wait for enthusiasm.

IN ONGOING RELATIONSHIPS:

(1) AVOID DOUBLE STANDARDS. It's OK if you and your spouse want different things, but *please* check it out. And don't do anything you wouldn't also want your partner to do. If a relationship is open, make it open on both sides. Give every freedom you want to take.

(2) HONESTY IS THE BEST POLICY. This is not the "let-me-be-perfectly-honest-with-you," vicious kind of honesty, but simple truth. None of us can be perfect with the truth, but most of us aren't doing as well as we could. If you have a long history of "cheating" (breaking agreements without prior renegotiation), resolve to clear it up. But be careful and give your partner a chance to adjust. Just blurting everything out may make things worse. If there's a big difference between the truth and what your agreement says, get counseling help to clear it up.

To clear up the confusion, choose a time when your relationship is going well, and suggest to your spouse that you haven't been entirely honest with him/her and that you want to clear it up. You might even ask him/her for what the best way to "break the news" would be. Suggest a counselor if you think you need one. No matter how hard it is, or no matter how much your spouse has said, "I couldn't stand it if you . . . ", breaking the news yourself is still going to be easier than if he/she finds it out by accident.

Also, allow your spouse some room for response. Don't insist that he/she take it calmly—he/she has a right to a reaction. Normally, if you give the reaction time to blow over, *then* things can be worked out.

This also applies to gay (and bisexual) men and women "coming out" to their parents (or even spouses). Remember, you have had time to get used to yourself. It probably wasn't too easy for you to accept at first, either. Your intimates also need some time to react before they'll be ready to work it out calmly. Parents and Friends of Lesbians and Gays, a wonderful nonprofit organization, puts out a booklet, "Read This Before Coming Out to Your Parents." The following sample is from their checklist:

QUESTIONS YOU NEED TO CONSIDER BEFORE COMING OUT

Are you sure about your sexual orientation? Don't raise the issue unless you're able to respond with confidence to the question, "Are you sure?" Confusion on your part will increase your parents' confusion and decrease their confidence in your judgment.

Do you have support? In the event your parents' reaction devastates you, there should be someone or a group that you can confidently turn to for emotional support and strength. Maintaining your sense of self-worth is critical.

Can you be patient? Your parents will require time to deal with this information if they haven't considered it prior to your sharing. The process may last from six months to two years.

The booklet is available free from PFLAG, Box 24565, Los Angeles, CA 90024. It contains twelve questions in all and lots of important information. I recommend it not only to gays coming out to parents, but also to bisexuals coming out to mates and/or family, and even to heterosexuals who are opening up to ultraconservative parents about a divorce or living together. It may even be helpful to someone who needs to tell the truth about infidelity to his/her partner.

Having the support of a counselor can be important. It can help you "wait out" the tough period before the acceptance. I've seen some very "hard-nosed," rigid people handle this sort of revelation quite well, once they had a chance to come to terms with it. Love is stronger than you can ever imagine.

(3) REMEMBER THAT THINGS CHANGE. We grow and change, we learn and re-evaluate. One of the kindest things you can do for yourself and your partner is to be able to handle change. This doesn't mean you have to like it, although you'd be surprised how often change does turn out for the better. Handle your own insecurities well enough to be able to see the positive aspects of change. Transition is always a shaky time, and if you've developed an inner support system, you'll deal with it much better. If change frightens you severely, you would greatly benefit from counseling before matters get out of hand.

Allow your relationship to let *you* know what it is, rather than attempting to make it conform to a predefined role. We all go through cycles, and so do our relationships. When Richard and I are in a time of separation, when we feel a little more distant, it helps a lot to know that it's just a cycle and that it will come around again to closeness *if we let it.*

(4) DO YOUR BEST TO FIND OUT WHAT'S GOING ON. Don't just assume you know, especially if what you "know" is negative. The other person in your life is not doing what he/she is doing *just to give you a hard time.* He/she is just making it through the day the best way possible, like you are. Give both of you a break, and if something looks irritating or frightening, check it out. Ask questions, say what you feel and ask whether your partner can relate. Seek to learn, because whatever the problem is, it can be solved with more information.

(5) REMEMBER YOU'RE FRIENDS. Your significant other is a dear friend, never your enemy. Be careful you're not treating him/her as if he/she were against you. Your partner has the same desire to get along that you do. If you let him/her know the easiest way to along with you, *and if you're willing to learn the easiest way to get along with your partner*, the struggle will dissolve. You are what you believe you are, and the more you focus on your friendship, the stronger the bonds will be.

(6) KEEP IN TOUCH. I highly recommend talking and sharing as a cure-all. Most of the time, if we'll just talk about it *and really listen*, we'll find the problem's not so big, after all. Set a frequent time and place for keeping in touch. Especially if you're living "on the leading edge" of creative relationships, you need that reinforcement often. If you want to make change smooth and easy, just keep talking. Frequent checking in on the progress being made minimizes the amount of new input you'll have to handle.

(7) DEVELOP A SUPPORT NETWORK. Especially when you live an "experimental" lifestyle, it's important to have support from others who are doing the same thing.

One of the benefits of counseling is the support it provides. As you explore new friendships, remember to gather and keep around you many ongoing friendships. "Make new friends, keep the old—one is silver, the other is gold": old wisdom, still appropriate today.

The society we live in is not supportive of experimental styles of living. You can always find someone who is frightened or self-righteous enough to put you down. The mass media promote lots of negative stereotypes that can hurt your self-image. So do yourself a favor and find people who think as you do, who'll support the positive and help you improve on the negative.

In a wonderful article on "Practical Friendship," John L. Hoff describes the power of friendship and relationship:

A friend is one
To whom one may pour
Out all the contents
Of one's heart,
Chaff and grain together,
Knowing that the
Gentlest of hands
Will take and sift it,
Keep what is worth keeping
And with a breath of kindness,
Blow the rest away.
            (Arabian proverb)

The conditions of modern society are hard on relationships. Our lives have become complex and stressful, making it difficult to nurture the spiritual connection between and among us that is called relationship. We are so preoccupied with seeing individuals as separate entities and assessing each other's different-ness that there is little sense of that which binds us, what we share in the context of relationship. Relationship is the most important context for our lives; it is the place where we really live, where we learn and grow. It is important to value our relationships and design them to be good environments for mutual growth. Yet so often our relationships are cold, tense, conflict-ridden, unfriendly environments. A simple way to say this is that the sense of *friendship* has been lost from our relationships.

Plato said, "Friendship is, strictly speaking, reciprocal benevolence, which inclines each party to be as solicitous for the welfare of the other as for his own." I would add to this that friendship is a strategy for personal growth; it involves a commitment to endure with each other and to make our lives and the world better through keeping each other healthily human and effectively loving. Relationships are our most precious resource. Knowing that, how do we value and utilize the resource of our relationships?

. . . Creating a circle of friends, that "mutual benevolence" of which Plato speaks, gives us both tangible assistance and a sense of being vitally connected with others . . . These experiments in practical friendships are resulting in many people becoming more open to their dreams of how life can really be—and in more people asking for help rather than remaining isolated and depressed . . . Our lives are our own dreams coming true, and our relationships are where we express our view of reality.

We need to know how to build relationships and how to use that field of force as an energy to nurture and guide us—it is our primary resource for human evolution and individual spiritual development. Relationship is an effective agent of change. It is in relationships that we collaborate with each other to create a better world. (*In Context*, Summer 1985.)

IMPORTANT INFORMATION FOR EVERYONE WHO EXPRESSES SEXUALLY IN ANY WAY:

(1) SEX, AIDS, VD AND CREATIVE RELATIONSHIPS. Today we are faced with a frightening development of the "sexual revolution": VD, herpes, AIDS, etc. All of us have been frightened, and the fear has been played upon by the media. The truth is that no one *has to* get a sexually transmitted disease.

First of all, disease does not jump out of dark corners and grab you when you're not looking. *You have to invite it!* The obvious answer is to learn to make disease unwelcome in your life, to invite good health instead.

If you're afraid of VD, herpes or AIDS, that could be an indication that you're recognizing you've made yourself vulnerable in some way. *Give this your immediate, healthy attention.* Make sure your health is good, that you're eating and sleeping well and that you're not engaging in unsafe sex practices, especially with persons you don't know well.

AIDS especially is quite simple to avoid. Most of the gay community has been very responsible and intelligent about changing sex practices, becoming informed and supporting each other. The bisexual and heterosexual communities could learn a valuable lesson from homosexuals. Sex is *not* necessarily dirty or unsafe. It's much like any other form of social intercourse. Be careful what you allow into your body, and your body will not be under attack.

Just as you can damage yourself with unhealthy food or choose to eat in a healthy manner, you have the same control over your sexuality.

You are not at the mercy of anyone else. When you practice safe sex and other good health measures, you take charge of your own health and take it out of the hands of others. This means you don't have to harass your partner about his/her sex practices. Just take charge of your own. If your partner wants sex without condoms, etc., then it's up to him/her to be trustworthy enough to inspire your confidence. When you feel unsure of your partner's practices, be very sure of your own.

This doesn't mean you can't have fun. Safe sex is just as much fun as unsafe sex; and without the added fear of contamination. *Be informed. Go to your local free clinic or community center and get tested.* Along with the testing, you'll be educated, which I see as far more important than the test. Richard has been tested every few months and has remained AIDS-free. Neither of us has ever been infected with a venereal disease, although we've both been sexually active and sexually experimental all of our adult lives.

Not long ago, Project Ahead, an AIDS education and control organization in Southern California, sponsored a day for staff and management personnel in the Long Beach Business Community, to help us learn the facts about AIDS. The seminar was taught by Ray Kincaid and Sunny Haberman.

Here are Project Ahead's guidelines for prevention:

Know your sex partners (this will reduce your stress as well as your chance of exposure).

Reduce the number of partners.

Use condoms (when properly used, they are very effective).

Don't use or share needles, razors, toothbrushes.

Avoid oral contact with fecal matter, semen and urine.

Stop or reduce the use of drugs, tobacco and alcohol (these are immune suppressants—use moderately. Also, antibiotics are *powerful* immune suppressants— use only when *absolutely* necessary, under your doctor's supervision, and don't hesitate to question your doctor about the necessity).

Most importantly, *keep your immune system strong and healthy:*

exercise regularly
eat a good balanced diet
get plenty of rest
reduce emotional stress.

This advice is as helpful for all other VD, including herpes, as it is for AIDS. None of these precautions are difficult, or require you to live joylessly. In fact, fun is a great disease preventer—it releases accumulated stress. If you know you aren't taking good care of your health, and you can't seem to change your habits, that's an issue for counseling. Get help with that before you seek help with your health.

You are equally entitled to sexual freedom and freedom from disease—don't make it an "either/or" choice! If you remember to think with your brain instead of your programmed guilt or your hormones, you'll be able to handle it well.

(2) IF YOU HAVE ALREADY BEEN EXPOSED. Having symptoms of VD, herpes, or AIDS or having a positive HTLV-III antibody test is frightening, not only because of the prognosis for your illness itself, but also because of the phobic reactions you experience, both in yourself and from the people around you. Most of us have considerable fear regarding these illnesses, some reasonable, some exaggerated.

There's no need to isolate yourself from society, friends and loved ones. That's self-punishment brought about by your own internal fears. It's not only unnecessary, but also bad for your emotional and physical health. Give yourself a chance to recover—make your life livable.

If you have one of the more drastic, longterm problems, there are many community groups and organizations to help and support you. Even if your family and friends have trouble supporting you, you're still not alone. Be open to some of the alternative forms of healing *in conjunction with accepted medical practice.* Most ethical doctors and holistic health practitioners are willing to work together, as long as they feel respected and considered.

Taking care of yourself includes safe sex. Become educated about your illness, get medical, psychological and spiritual help and find out what "safe sex" is for you. Remember, it's unhealthy for you to be re-exposed to the illness, or to a different illness—not to mention how emotionally stress-ful it is to feel badly about exposing others.

Talk about it. Let people know what's going on with you *before* taking any possible risks, and *always* practice safe sex. There is no need for you to be isolated, as long as you act responsibly. Affection, hugging, conversation and general closeness are not dangerous. They can only help you heal.

Please understand that in this chapter I've used the term "etiquette" loosely. The point is, we need some guidelines to go by. I hope you'll find the above ideas useful, and I urge you to think about compiling your own guidelines. We need more than these!

CHAPTER FOUR

BEING YOURSELF IN SOCIETY

AFTER ALL THIS TALK ABOUT individuality and the importance of your own wants and needs, I feel the need to seek a balance by putting it all in the context of the society in which we live. There's been a lot of confusion lately, with nasty things being said about the "Me Generation" which I tend to take personally.

Actually, *everything* seeks a balance, and because we were so out of balance for so long in not recognizing the power and importance of the self, we then got rather out of balance in the other direction. A healthy self-image is essential to good relationships, and a healthy society can only be based on healthy individuals who in turn will produce future healthy individuals. It's a chicken-or-the-egg question: Which do we handle first, the health of the individual, or the health of the group?

Actually, in real life, we handle both at the same time, and we work on both ends until we meet in the middle. The same is true in a relationship. The unhealthy aspects of a relationship reflect and contribute to the emotionally unhealthy aspects of the people involved, and vice versa. By the same reasoning, the health of the individuals promotes the health of the relationship, and vice versa.

The truth is, we can only love others as much as we are capable of loving ourselves, for that is our essential role model for how the world is, and how to love.

In an article called, "Self-Image and Self-Love: The Key to Romance," Catherine Solange puts it this way:

> Self-love is *attractive!* Research on body language and first impressions shows that people decide if they "like" you in less than four minutes, even without verbal exchange. What information do you give out in those first four minutes? Without even saying a word, you are telling the world how much you like yourself and your life.

> "Whatever you radiate you attract" is a well-known principle. You can think of the quality of your thoughts and feelings about yourself as establishing a certain frequency around you. The quality of others' thoughts and feelings toward you can only come in on your frequency. If what you experience in your love life is lots of rejection, you may want to ask, "How am I rejecting myself?" Self-rejection simultaneously attracts rejecting partners and invalidates potentially loving partners. (*L.A. Resources,* Fall 1985.)

However, this does *not* make self-love more important than love of others. We're back to the Golden Rule: "Love thy neighbor *as thyself.*"

The truth is, we need each other. That is fine and healthy as long as we also recognize that we need *ourselves* too. Even if we don't like the environment or the group system, we cannot change it from the *outside*. Attacking a system from the outside (telling them what's wrong with *them*) does not work. The members of the system will simply unite against the attack, and the system, even if it's un-healthy, will be strengthened by the attack. (I know that be-fore long our world political leaders will "get" this powerful idea!)

From *inside* the system, however, the situation is different. If the system (or persons) defines you as "member," "friend" or "loved one," your word, your opinions immedi-ately gain immense weight and power. Just stop and think it over. Who do *you* listen to? Is it easier to hear criticism and count it important when it's said by a stranger whom you regard as "having no right" to say it? Or is it easier to hear it when said gently with love by a respected and ad-mired friend?

Even if you've been an accepted member of a family or group, but you offer your criticism without love and accep-tance of the people involved, you become, temporarily, an outsider, a person not to be heeded, but to be defended against.

So, no matter how right, how spiritual, how healthy you feel, you must consider your *effectiveness*. In order to be ef-fectively heard, at times patience is called for. It's often necessary to win the acceptance of the majority before you begin to create change.

All of this is merely to say, as one friend to another, please don't offend people with your lifestyle, your ideals and dreams, and life will be much easier on you. (A friend tells me that a teacher named Thorin says, "Be in the world, but not of it—and don't spook the natives!" A wonderful way to express the same idea!)

There is plenty of time to accomplish your goal if you remain aware of your effectiveness. No person, group, family or nation can resist enough persistent and clear love.

Hang in there gently. Use the reaction of the group as your guide. You can tell what they perceive of you by their response. Make corections as you go along. With enough gentleness and love, you can get away with outrageous things! Be open to correction, or a better idea—and don't give up! With perseverance and patience, mountains can indeed be moved. Hang in there for your beliefs and your dreams. The rewards are worth the effort.

Chapter Five

SAMPLE LOVESTYLES/ LIFESTYLES

THIS IS THE PART I'VE been waiting for! Asking my friends to contribute to this book has pointed out to me how profoundly my own life is surrounded with love and caring. Reading these generous sharings of what these people normally keep private and protected has moved me. I hope you can overcome any shock and/or judgment that may arise in you, so that you can experience the love expressed here.

The point of all this is to give people who otherwise would have no way of knowing about them a look at the variety of possibilities in relationships and some role models. Hopefully, someone who fears what he/she wants in love will be reassured by discovering that different people need different lives.

There are many more lifestyles available than are represented here. This is just a tiny sample of the possibilities, limited to the people who were willing to write for me.

These people are sharing their private lives with you in order to shed light on ignorance and help make a place in the world for creativity in loving. Hopefully, together we'll increase the energy in the world for acceptance and tolerance. To all of my friends who were so generous with their time and their privacy, again I say a heartfelt thanks.

SHAKTI GAWAIN

Shakti Gawain is not a personal friend of mine, a fact that I hope will change. I know her through her books, Creative Visualization *(Whatever Publishing, 1978) and* Living in the Light *(Whatever Publishing, 1986). I recommend them both highly. The following is excerpted from* Living in the Light, *which she co-wrote with Laurel King:*

"For me, the commitment I make is to myself—to love, honor, obey, and cherish my own being. My commitment in a relationship is to truth and honesty. To anyone I love I promise to do the best I can to tell the truth, to share my feelings, to take responsibility for myself, to honor the connection I feel with that person, and to maintain that connection, no matter how the form may change.

"Real commitment makes no guarantees about a relationship's form; real commitment allows for the fact that form is constantly changing, and that we can trust that process of change. It opens the door to the true intimacy that is created when people share deeply and honestly with one another. If two people stay together on this basis, it's because they really want to be together. They continue to find an intensity of love and learning with each other as they change and grow.

Monogamous and Nonmonogamous Relationships

"When people first hear my views on relationships, they

may find them rather radical, and perhaps they are. Often, however, I find in talking to them further that they have misunderstood certain things that I'm saying. For example, sometimes people think I am "against monogamy"—that I am advocating nonmonogamous relationships. This is definitely not the case. What I am advocating is truth— being honest with your feelings and responses, being true to yourself.

"Some people I know are truly involved in a monogamous relationship. They have one powerful, primary sexual/ romantic connection and no desire for any others. A few seem to be strongly nonmonogamous and have little trouble handling more than one sexual/romantic relationship. Most people experience some degree of mixed feelings and conflict on this issue. They want depth, closeness, and security with one person; they feel guilty about being attracted to others; and they feel threatened by their partner being attracted to anyone else. On the other hand, they feel somewhat restricted and sometimes wish they could be free to explore other connections. Those who are involved in many relationships may also have a deep longing to find one person they want to be with exclusively.

"These feelings are an important part of our human conditioning and need to be felt and acknowledged, at least to ourselves, and preferably to our loved ones as well. The conflicts are automatically dissolved as we learn to simply accept and trust ourselves. The real issue is not the external form of our relationships—that is resolved easily and effortlessly as we learn to trust and follow our own inner truth. Each person will create the relationships that are exactly right for him- or herself and for everyone else concerned.

"I am finding that being alive is a love affair with the universe. I also think of it as a love affair between my inner male and female, and between my form and my spirit.

"As I build and open my channel, more and more energy flows through. I feel greater intensity of feeling and passion. Being in love is a state of being not dependent on any one person. However, certain people attract me and seem to intensify or deepen my experience of the life force within me. I know that those people are mirrors to me and also that they are channels for special energy in my life.

"I move toward them because I want the intensification that I experience with them. I feel the universe moving through me to them, and moving through them to me. This could happen through any form of exchange—talking, touching, making love. The energy itself lets me know what is needed and appropriate. It's a mutually satisfying and fulfilling exchange because the universe is giving each of us what we need. It may be a brief, one-time experience, a glance or a short conversation with a stranger. Or it may be an ongoing contact, a profound relationship that lasts for many years. I see it more and more as the universe coming to me constantly, through many different channels.

"What I have just written is an ideal scene. I certainly am not living it fully at every moment. Many times I am caught up in my fears and relationship addictions. However, I *am* experiencing it more and more frequently, and when I do, it feels wonderful!"

SHIRLEY MACLAINE

Another woman I admire, although I don't personally know

her, is Shirley MacLaine. The following is from her best-selling book, Out on a Limb *(Bantam, 1984), and describes her experience with a creative lifestyle which worked for her, and which was transitory. Here she talks about its effect on herself and her daughter:*

"Climbing my long driveway I felt the low-hanging cherry trees brush the top of my car. I loved those trees. They reminded me of the cherry trees my former husband Steve and I had had in his house in Japan before our divorce. Steve had planted them there when he lived in a residential section of Tokyo called Shibuya. He wanted to stay and live and work in and around Asia. I wanted to live and work in America, not because I grew up there, but because my work was there. We discussed the dilemma and decided to try to make the globe a golf ball and do both.

"For a while it worked. But gradually we each developed separate lives. We remained friends as we raised our daughter Sachi, who spent the first seven years of her life with me in America, the next six in an international school in Japan, and her remaining school years in Switzerland and England. She learned to speak and read and write fluent Japanese (which meant she could read most any Oriental language) and she began to *think* and *perceive* like an Oriental). . . .

"I learned a lot about Asia from Sachi which she didn't even mean to teach me. She is one of that new breed of people whose blood and ancestry is Western, but whose psychology and thought processes are half Asian. With Sachi this was a result of the "golf-ball" belief that Steve and I had had in the beginning. As with everything, it has its duality—its drawbacks and its assets. In the long run, though, I would say the assets outweigh the liabilities, if for no other reason than the fact that Sachi is a combination of two worlds—and if she can handle it, she will help each understand the other."

DEBORAH ANAPOL

Deborah Anapol, Ph.D. in clinical psychology, specializes in the design of new family structures. She is founder of the nonprofit educational organization INTINET, whose purpose is to link and support people who are pioneering longterm, inclusive, sexualove relationships. For more information write to her at Star Route Box 312, Sausalito, CA 94965.

The following is from an article in In Context *magazine, Summer 1985.*

Polygamy: Another Lovestyle

by Deborah Anapol

OPENING THE WAY FOR DIVERSITY OF FORM IN HEALTHY RELATIONSHIPS

"Sometime in the fall of 1983 I had a startling insight. It gave coherence to my relationship history, including my two failed marriages. It resolved my lifelong sense that my sexual feelings were at once wonderful and out of sync with accepted social norms. It incorporated my professional focus on the flaws in family structure which spawn epidemic wife-beating and child abuse. It freed me from over 5 years of scrutinizing my internal and external worlds, looking for what was wrong. Suddenly, in a flash, nothing was wrong! Everything made sense. And it was so simple: I HAD

232

BEEN A POLYGAMOUS WOMAN ALL MY LIFE, TRYING TO FIT MYSELF INTO A MOLD THAT NEITHER FIT ME NOR MY PERCEPTION OF THE TIMES I WAS LIVING IN. After more than a decade of struggling with relationship issues, I saw that the trouble might well be less with me (or with my partners or with not choosing or being chosen by the 'right' partner) than it was with a simple mismatch between me and monogamy, or the institution of marriage as we know it.

"My professional training, my spiritual education and my personal philosophy all pointed in the opposite direction—that maturity and peace came with tempering the will through acceptance of and skillful working with the realities of one's circumstances. Yet my insight and my gut rang with the truth that the circumstance called *monogamy* and *marriage* was what needed to bend. And possibly for more couples than just me.

THE PAST

"I scanned my sexual and relationship history from the point of view of a polygamous and sexually awake woman moving through a monogamous and generally sexually repressed world . . . [Here Deborah reviews her two past marriages: her first marriage ended when her daughter was born, and her husband felt like a 'second child' to her; her second marriage she describes and evaluates as follows:]

"As I see it now, this second marriage was a classic case of relationship-as-an-end-in-itself. We had no common goal or shared purpose for our relationship other than our own family. His number one priority was to preserve the relationship; my number one priority was to perfect myself and create a better world. We were at cross purposes. He wanted me to grow, but he also feared that the relationship could not survive or contain my expansion. And he was right.

More than One

"And then I looked at my most recent relationships. Quite by 'accident' I met five different men within the space of a month who became my lovers. It felt wonderful to exchange this much love. And, quite by 'accident,' they were all into nonexclusive, nonpossessive relationships, so there was no conflict over expectations or demands. They were all very different from each other, and they each brought something unique to our relationship. I had given up looking for one man who had it all.

"Slowly they met each other, and I met their other lovers. We got a taste of what it would be like to be part of a network where everyone was a lover. We delighted in giving each other the gift of new friends. Eventually I began to long for deeper commitment, more sharing. I wanted us all to live together—but not all of us connected on every level, not all of us had identical visions. So, we drifted apart . . . but this was an important piece in my relationship puzzle.

Another Way?

"As I scanned these 'facts' from my past, I wondered . . . could this recent experience be the new mating behavior of polygamous people? Might we be seeking to expand our committed relationships through this love-network, and not merely be 'hedonists' who are 'unable to make commitments'? Might there be a higher level of integration and relationship being born while monogamy and marriage and family are seeming to disintegrate? Might the urge to bond with many like-minded beings on many levels—including the sexual—be an expression of humanity's growing spiritual awareness?

"I came to understand and accept myself as a polygamous woman. It was just a fact for me that anyone I love I want to have sex with. It seemed crazy to legislate loving only one person, especially when there may be many polygamous people out there. Loving another person doesn't mean you stop loving the first—not if it's a high-quality connection. What a terrible burden to place on a person: to be the one for whom he/she forsook all others. The real difficulty of polygamy is the time it takes to relate to more people deeply. But it also frees time from internal (domestic) and external (economic) functions.

"Monogamy for me had been an uncomfortable either/or balancing act—freedom *or* intimacy, flexibility *or* loyalty, change *or* commitment. Polygamy had given me a framework for how to integrate these polarities in a responsible way. Stability *and* excitement. Security *and* freedom. Intimacy *and* inclusiveness. Depth *and* diversity. . .

"My professional self entered the internal review. If polygamy were an accepted relationship form in our society, might it ease some of the deep social problems of, on the one hand, family violence and disintegration and, on the other hand, the alienation of the maritally disenfranchised —the lonely single? Again, the response was yes, *yes!*

"If we really want to save the family we must expand its boundaries. There is a strength in numbers. What function does it serve to *insist* on monogamy? It keeps the family weak, contracted and unsteady because it is always vulnerable to the threat of loss. With monogamy, if Mom or Dad should love another, they could not be included in the family—they must *replace* the spouse. Destroy the family. Divorce. Why is adultery as grounds for divorce such a given?

"In a larger group, an individual may leave temporarily—or permanently—for career/emotional/personal reasons without destroying the family. Parents can get time off. Dependency, while destructive, is often the glue of bonding, keeping people together when conflict, friction and challenges come up. In polygamy, dependency is diffused, spread between several adults, thus lessening the burden on any one person.

"As families become smaller with Zero Population Growth, the adult-to-child ratio goes up, but children lose the opportunity to have siblings. Extended families or clans would give these children brothers and sisters . . .

"I now know that many people are experimenting with and actualizing relationships, marriages, and sexuality that go beyond the couple. They are discovering what works and what doesn't; they have found routes beyond jealousy and possessiveness, beyond dependency and insecurity, beyond ignorance, fear and guilt in their sexuality . . . but they are not sharing this vital information publicly for fear of being judged. They are wary of the loss of respect and credibility both *from* the alternative community and *for* the alternative community. This silence perpetuates the illusions that: (1) only the Moral Majority is concerned about the crisis in the family; (2) most people are satisfied with and find fulfillment in exclusive couple/nuclear arrangements; (3)

the experiments of the 60s and 70s are a thing of the past, a dead-end; (4) anyone who prefers multi-partner relationships is either immature and immoral or (worse yet) unrealistic and idealistic; and (5) it is improper to openly discuss our emotional, sexual, and physical needs, desires and solutions in ways which allow us to learn from each other, draw closer to each other and leave the tyranny of habit behind. . . .

"When I encounter my fears, I remind myself . . . there is a part of me which is wiser, stronger, more truthful, more creative and more courageous than the everyday self I have been taught to present to the world. This self emerges at critical moments with solutions which rise above the apparent paradoxes which I experience as blocks. I have learned to trust it as the most enlightened part of myself. And this self is a polygamist."

MAGGIE AND EDDIE (from Maggie's point of view)

Maggie has been my dear, dear friend and "sister" for twenty years. She and I have been through many changes together, much growth and many fun times. At one time, I was the monogamously married one, and she was the "wild single woman." Now she's living an almost-traditional lifestyle, with the main "nontraditional" ingredient being that she runs her own business from her home.

Through all the changes, our connection has remained strong. The differences in our lifestyles have never been a serious problem to our friendship, and whatever we face in the future, I'm certain we'll face it with each other. Maggie, her husband and adopted baby daughter are also experimenting with "open adoption," in which the child's "birth mother" also has access to the baby as she grows.

My lifestyle: I am a thirty-nine-year-old woman, married, with one child, a very special daughter, five months old, a wondrous cat and a very large, lovely eight-month-old puppy. We live in the suburbs in a single house. My week-days are spent caring for the baby and working at my book-keeping service part-time. I have childcare in my home while I work. Playtime is spent reading, relaxing with my family and friends, going out visiting or to a restaurant. The overall image I have of my lifestyle is a warm, loving envi-ronment centered around my immediate family, enriched and expanded to my friends and extended family.

My lovestyle has many facets to me. I express love by say-ing "I love you," by doing helpful things, by reaching out to touch with love, giving gifts, telephoning, visiting, listen-ing. I receive love with enjoyment and appreciation. My lovestyle is verbal and active.

My lovestyle fits my lifestyle well, with lots of opportuni-ties each day to express my love to my husband, child, friends and family, and to receive love back.

I find my current lifestyle overall satisfying. The arrival of our child five months ago has created major changes in my lifestyle. Primarily, I went from a full-time career person to a full-time mommy and a part-time career person. I gave up a lot of spontaneity and sleep! Although the change was major, it was anticipated and wanted. The adjustments have been gradual and evolving. It feels real easy to be able to express my love in my "style" on a daily basis—by caring for my daughter, playing and interacting with her, by caring for my mate actively (preparing meals, doing errands, wel-coming him home each evening). I enjoy having opportu-nities to see and talk to friends and other family members.

I would like to have more time for me. I'm not actively doing anything to gain more time for myself right now. I believe that as my daughter grows older and more independent, I will have more time for me.

I do think that I have had a very long journey figuring out what would work for me. Part of the reason that this journey has been so long is that my needs and desires have changed as I matured. I see my major struggle as not being able to realize a deep desire (to become pregnant) for many years. The lesson seems to have been enjoy "today" instead of living for the future. I am not sure what would have made it easier.

My current lifestyle/lovestyle would not have suited me at an earlier time in my life. My needs have evolved throughout my adult life. I began with needing excitement, change, uncertainty and lots of variety. As I grew and developed, I settled into needing more stability and commitment and less uncertainty. The process has been gradual, but I think I have evolved to a very different current style when compared to my early adult life twenty or so years ago.

As I progressed through my life, my changes in style have meant a change in partners. In my earlier adult life, my partners reflected my needs for uncertainty and resistance to commitment. Some of the bigger changes in my style were made without a partner. My commitment to my current partner came after a period of a couple of years without a partner, during which time I did a lot of growth work about what I wanted in a relationship. I have been together with my current partner for eleven years. This relationship has evolved and changed and deepened greatly. I think it is significant, though, that we came into this partnership with similar basic wants. The ease I feel in this relationship today is a reflection of our use of communication to each other of our separate styles. This communication led to changes in each of our styles which allowed us to feel more loved and valued by each other.

ELIZABETH AND DAN (From Elizabeth's point of view)

This wonderful lady is a family woman with her own business teaching exercise classes.

My lifestyle changes month by month, dictated by the needs of my family. My primary role: I'm the one who nurtures. Recent family needs (my mother, sister, son) took a lot of my time and energy.

My time is used in seven major areas:

(1) Serving the emotional needs of my family.

(2) Fulfilling the requirements of my part-time business. It is my creative outlet, fulfills my need to socialize and is an ego boost, so it's definitely an important part of my life.

(3) Maintenance of my home. I don't enjoy this much. I used to feel mad all the while I was cleaning. Cutting down on housework has definitely improved my lifestyle. But—I love a clean, shiny house, so I do it!

(4) Household business. My husband (Dan) and I take turns being the bill-payer on alternative years, but I make the appointments for *everything* (Doctors, vet, home repairs, etc.). This is my *least* favorite output of time; still, I learned that doing all this stuff is better than letting it slide.

(5) Shopping, storing, preparing and serving food. This takes lots of time, but I enjoy the whole process.

(6) Driving people places. I do it a lot.

(7) My self time. I love to read, for pleasure and to keep up on my business. Also, a good cup of coffee and about twenty minutes of TV is a great pleasure. Twenty minutes seems to satisfy me.

This lifestyle brings me satisfaction—further than contented, all the way to *happy!* Most days are happy. I see all my activities as a big, bright bouquet, and I'm fortunate enough to be holding it, inhaling it, experiencing it. There's a weed or two and some brown petals, but still all acceptable and nice.

My lovestyle: I show my love to my family and husband first by caring physically and emotionally about them. I am not good at providing financially or at discipline or training. Other traits of my lovestyle are: kindness; honesty (real important; but "soft" honesty—positive whenever possible); showing my humor and appreciating theirs; being there (I have worked part-time so I could be available); accepting (all kinds of things—crazy clothes and hair; Dan's not wanting to socialize; his becoming a gardner instead of the artist I married—I understood he felt he was selling his soul); listening and understanding; using helpful, not hurtful words. Most of my lovestyle involves feelings and service.

Dan and I have a lovestyle that goes thick and thin, depending on outside demands. Luckily, when we've gone through our most difficult circumstances is when we stand together the thickest, when we can totally count on each other to do anything of a loving and supporting nature. We'll use totally foreign behavior if that's what we need to get through. We, who are usually pretty private about our relationship with God, have held hands and prayed aloud back and forth for help and strength in a crisis.

We share something that may be unusual: a sense of detachment, as though we were *behind* the camera, and the world's a stage. It's added a dimension of appreciation, even gratefulness, for each experience we've had—even the most commonplace daily events. I also suspect it has protected us through some painful times.

Our circumstances have required different strengths at differet times, and we have been poles apart in some areas and stages. Eventually, we come back together.

I have learned to expect change. I've been poor, comfortable and (moderately) rich. Comfortable strikes the best balance for me. Dan prefers "rich," but he's getting tired of the price of getting there. Poor and rich are both too costly in our case.

I am preparing in small ways for my family to need me less as the children grow up. I want to increase the time I spend with friends, in study and discussion groups. Dan likes involvement in politics, but I don't. I'm also preparing for full-time employment; taking the first step by returning to school.

My basic personality has not changed much from childhood, but society has. I've dropped the idea that spouses have to have lots of togetherness to be happy, that families *must* have dinner together, that a home must be spotless, that problems are bad.

I feel loved and loving. I am grateful to be in harmony with my own morality. I love the opportunities to use my skills and talents. I'm in control as a self-employed woman. I allow my life to be adjusted to my family's needs, but I know I can say *no* if I choose. I also realize that the ultimate control I have over whatever comes my way is that I choose my reaction. I feel financially secure. I have good health.

Upon rereading this, I'm saying, "Who is this saintly, loving woman? My family would like to meet her!" What's missing is time pressure. When my tight schedule goes awry, the patience and kindness often go out the window, and anger bubbles in my soul. Dan is the one who feels this most, as he is the one I let down with—he deserves better.

Also, I left out my absolute bullheadedness about *really big issues!* When I wanted to move, and Dan didn't, I announced our move to all our friends and told Dan privately he had no choice. I would take my 50% of our property and move. He'd lose his lifestyle anyway, so he might as well come along. He did.

At another time, when I felt I was carrying the whole load of a family (teenager) crisis while Dan was involved in a neighborhood civic issue, he insisted I was making a mountain out of a molehill. So, I moved out! After two days, he realized the gravity of the situation at home and began arranging counseling, etc., but not before I told him I'd *never* come home if he didn't take over.

There. That's a more balanced and truthful picture.

ELDON AND BILL (from Eldon's point of view)

These men have a long-standing, loving, solid relationship, and both are very active in (you might say pillars of) the gay

243

community in the city where we live. As good friends, we see each other often, and, except for the gender of the partners, this relationship seems very "traditional":

My lifestyle is, for the most part, comfortably middle-class. I was born and raised in the Midwest (Kansas) and was an only child. I was raised in small towns, received a B.A. degree from a church-supported college in Oklahoma, and an M.A. degree from Kansas State University.

I moved to California in 1976, after working four years as a program director for a Cable TV station and as a manager of a movie theater. One important aspect of my lifestyle is that I am gay, and that is the main reason I moved out of the Midwest.

I am now owner of my own business, which is in its eighth year, and co-owner of a small corporation, which is less than a year old. I publish a business directory for the local gay/ lesbian community and am co-publisher of a gay/lesbian-oriented magazine and newspaper for all of Southern California. I am happy and pleased with my current lifestyle.

My lovestyle is rather conservative, and I have been with my current (and only) lover for nearly ten years. We met shortly after I moved to California, courted a few months later (candlelight dinners, theatre, moonlight walks, etc.) and have been living together since January of 1977.

My lover had been married for twenty-six years, has three grown children, and had been divorced for less than a year (but had separated from his wife for nearly two years). In July of 1978, we celebrated our Holy Union in an MCC Church. (A Holy Union is a service of commitment and dedication between two men or two women, and the service is similar to a traditional heterosexual wedding; however, it is *not* legally sanctioned in any state.)

My parents were not very physically demonstrative, and I do not recall many tender moments between my mother and father. However, it was a comfortable environment, and I was not neglected, abused, or deprived.

I, on the other hand, am very affectionate (a quality or trait which seemed natural to me in my encounters with other men, but which was not expressed, in any degree, with myself and my parents). My mother used to hug me before I left for college, and my father embraced and hugged me for the first time just before I moved to California. My lover was not so affectionate (a result, he says, of the last years of his marriage), but has changed as our relationship has grown and has improved greatly.

I feel that both my current lifestyle and lovestyle are very satisfying. One of the most important things in *any* type of relationship (love, business, friend, or whatever) is *communication!* My lover, in the first couple of years of our relationship, was quiet and withdrawn. If something was bothering him, he would brood about it and keep it to himself. After enough questioning on my part, he would open up and talk about what was bothering him.

We now have a good level of communication, and my lover has said that one of the things for which he is most grateful in our relationship is that I caused him to "come out of his shell" and communicate his feelings. I am very fortunate to also have good mutual communication with my business partner on all business matters (that sure helps to make my lifestyle happier).

There are a few things I would like to change about my lifestyle (such as becoming more organized at the office and at home), but I am working on them, and in time *may* change! I can't think of anything in my lovestyle I would like to change. My lover is very sentimental, and I like to surprise him from time to time (no special occasion) with flowers, a nice love-note or card or a small gift. I also try to tell him, at least once a day, "I Love You!"

I don't recall a "struggle" or "long journey" to find out what would work for me, but everything has seemed, with the grace of God, to fall into place (sometimes more easily than other times, however). My lover and I are both religious, attend church regularly, and believe that God has played an important part in our lives and our happiness.

RILEY AND RHODA (from Riley's point of view)

I've been with Riley through many relationship changes. We like to say "we grew up together," even though we were both over thirty when we met. This relationship is relatively new, and it's great to see them develop their mutual lovestyle. Both are licensed therapists.

Our similarities brought us together and our differences make us learn and laugh. We struggled at first—mostly out of fear that we were too different to make it work. Rhoda is Jewish-American from Detroit and I am a WASP from Texas.

We knew we were OK when, one sunny day about three months after we moved in together, we were having lunch in our back yard. She was eating tofu and vegetables and sipping herbal tea and I was eating a bacon sandwich and regular iced tea. Rho looked at our food, looked at me and said, "I guess we're incompatible." We both laughed. And laughed and laughed. Because we knew then that it didn't matter.

There have been time when we would entertain each other doing Jewish-WASP jokes to the degree that I once commented that even if our material was hilarious, we'd never make it on stage because it was in such bad taste.

Rho is pushy. To me, a full-fledged WASP, pushy is not OK. A WASP only pushes when pushed and he can't stand pushy people. She asks for the booth she wants in restaurants. She'll send back food that isn't right. She returns gifts she doesn't like to the store where they were purchased—without a receipt, yet!

I'm sometimes aghast and sometimes in awe, but it didn't take me long to figure out that Rho really knows how to get what she wants and that I can learn from her. I even ask her to push for me sometimes.

At home she asks me to do something she wants done—like water the plants she planted last week. Sometimes I don't want to, or I'm busy and I say no. *And she argues with me!* Unthinkable!

I'm left with the choice of giving in or standing my ground. Since I know we won't like each other if I give in, I stand my ground and push back. That's fairly new for me and, I'll tell you, it feels great! I'm learning to push. I'm learning that pushing is a very useful skill to have sometimes. I mean, I can be downright thankful that Rho is who she is.

MATT AND BERT

Matt and Bert have done an exceptional job of sharing their styles. The only thing they haven't mentioned is what delightful people they are, and how they always seem to energize a room just by being in it. The following is exactly as they gave it to me:

MATT

My wife Bert (for Bertha) and I are one of the happiest couples I know. Bert is 68 and I am 66. We met eleven years ago at a nudist camp in Pennsylvania. We started dating the next year. Three years later we started living together and in two more years we married. Two months after the marriage, I retired and we moved from Philadelphia to Long Beach, California. Our life is one of retirement, in which we leisurely pursue our various interests, including socializing, some travel, going to cultural events, reading, enjoying our video collection and generally welcoming each new day. We wrote our own marriage ceremony and included in it the fact that we are both feminists and that ours is an "open" lifestyle, in which we are both free to develop intimate relationships with others. I want to try to explain why we are so happy.

I think that the key to Bert's and my success is that we both pretty much accept ourselves and each other as is. Neither of us is trying to improve or change the other in any way. This means that we are really willing to let the other do whatever he or she wants. Or course, we know each other well enough so that we know each other's general wants pretty well. However, on a day-to-day basis neither of us pressures the other to do anything, whether it is sharing a walk, eating at the same time, shopping together or having sex. We live in a kind of mutual state of high enjoyment of each other's company. At the same time, as I will elaborate below, we are free to enjoy fully other people. Neither of us, however, wants to spend much time away from the other doing this. However, if either should want to make a trip back East, he or she would respect the other's desire to go or not to go.

Another major factor in Bert's and my rapport is that we share so many of the same interests. This might seem surprising in view of our different backgrounds. I am black; Bert is white. I am a Harvard Law School graduate; Bert is a high-school graduate, having graduated from Mooseheart, the Moose Lodge's school for children of Moose members who have died. I grew up in the normal "nuclear family" situation; Bert from ages 7–17 grew up in a boarding school, where her mother worked elsewhere on the premises. In any event both Bert and I are what I would call humanitarian liberals. We see human beings as basically good and favor a form of government which encourages and nourishes the personal development of all its citizens. We abhor the kind of militaristic nationalism that encourages people to view people of various other nations as something less than human beings trying to learn how to live. We would like to see a government which guarantees all our citizens certain basics, like employment and medical care. Culturally, our interests are very similar. We both love books, plays, movies, concerts and ballet. Neither of us is a sports fan. We both are people people; we love to socialize and are attracted to the same people.

Both Bert and I approach life head-first. By that I mean that we are inclined to analyze our problems and then do what our heads tell us is best. If our emotions do not feel happy with our intellectual decisions, we nevertheless implement these decisions with a fair try. If our emotions continue to complain, we will then review the decision. However, neither one of us is a person who feels his or her way through life, trying to find circumstances that "feel right." Neither of us would be inclined to make a decision that our emotions seemed to favor, but which did not seem sensible to our minds. This common approach makes communication relatively easy for us. I should add that, at this stage of our lives, neither Bert nor I are very problem-oriented. We have no major goals we are striving for. There are no changes in our lives we feel pressed to make. We love Southern California and enjoy each day here. We have good friends on both coasts and we make more each year.

Interestingly, Bert's and my lovestyles are very similar, though our sex styles are inclined to be different. We both enjoy telling each other that we love each other. We both are very genuinely interested in seeing the other pleased. We love to touch each other. We are always patting each other as we pass around the house. We both love to cuddle in bed. Indeed, our bed is our headquarters. We watch TV, read, snack and converse in it. We love to share our bed with others, too. It is eighty inches wide (a non-California king), and many singles and a few couples have snuggled with us in it. When it comes to sex, I am inclined to put more emphasis on its generic aspect and Bert is more inclined to emphasize the special aspect. For Bert sex is really 99% making love with me. For her it seems to me that sex is primarily a celebration of our couplehood. Although she is very responsive physically, I have the feeling that it is still not a compelling need with her, compared to the need to touch and feel close to me. As a result Bert is not particularly interested sexually in other men, though there are a small few she enjoys being with sexually from time to time.

I am more inclined to view sex in terms of my basic maleness meeting a woman's basic femaleness. The fact that a woman is sexually interested in a lot of men is a stimulating factor for me. Also sex for me is very much an interest (mental) as well as an activity (physical). The beauty of Bert's and my open relationship is that neither of us has to be everything to the other sexually. I thoroughly enjoy and love Bert's sense of celebration of our relationship physically. Making love to her is certainly making love. On the other hand I am also free to enjoy women with a different orientation, often in Bert's presence. I have several good female sexual friends. However, I do not have any pattern of contact with them and do not feel a need for one. On the contrary, one of the problems of open-relating, if one's relationships become too structured, is that they tend to conflict. As it is, the whole arrangement works smoothly and without any compulsiveness. All the women I am interested in are really dear friends of both Bert and me. Bert's appreciation of my sexual needs and interests makes her an ideal partner for me, even if our personal lovestyles are somewhat different. Every time I make love to another woman, it is as if I were receiving a gift from Bert too, a gift that enriched our relationship.

Bert and I have no fears of either rejecting the other. It would make no sense for either of us to give up a relationship that is so gratifying. (Our heads having concluded this, our feelings don't worry about a thing.) We do not "work on" our relationship, because we do not feel any need to. We do indeed take it for granted, in the sense that we unequivocally expect it to last our joint lives. I personally cannot conceive of any ideal person I would rather live with than Bert. Not only do I feel my love flowing out to her all the time, but I also feel her love flowing to me. It makes no difference whether it is expressed with pats, looks, words or no conduct at all; it is always there. I feel that Bert shares my own sense of vitality, however I wish to express it, and that is a very heart-warming feeling.

When my wife and I married five years ago, we wrote our own wedding ceremony and included the following language: "We like to think of our relationship as inclusive, rather than exclusive. We conceive of it as a loving circle into which others may be drawn. We have also experienced being drawn into the loving circles of others. From the beginning we have had a relationship in which each of us has been free to pursue our vital interests. This has included the development of intimate relationships with others, sometimes including sexual expression. The key to openness and inclusiveness, however, is not physical touching, but rather the speaking of one human heart to other human hearts. We are attracted to similar people and our past relationship has been enriched by our inclusion of others. We do not intend that marriage alter this rewarding pattern."

BERT

Matt has done a very good job describing our life- and lovestyles and how compatible they are. It is wonderful to arrive at retirement as a new bride and to share and grow with a partner who is so easy to live, love and laugh with and who gives such practical and loving support through the rough times—a serious illness of mine and the death of my youngest daughter early in the second year of our marriage.

Our open loving-circle life- and lovestyles seem to fit us perfectly, adding to and enriching each one's life. I think such styles are particularly suited to mature men and women of any age, whether married or single.

I married at age twenty and, as Tina would put it, thought we had just added another candle, not blown our own out. This was back in the 30s and there were not too many marriage counselors around, so we had our own in-house system. By agreement—no silent treatment, no running home for me (my husband was an only child whose parents were both dead), coming out honestly with our feelings. My husband had grown up on a farm with an imaginary playmate named Joe. Joe came with the marriage and let us settle so many things with humor. It was so easy to turn to the imaginary Joe and ask his opinion of what the other had said or done, letting each other hear our complaints in a nonthreatening manner. Our marriage was open in every way but sexually, and I must confess I didn't know anyone who had a sexually open one or who cheated. Our happy, satisfying marriage ended with his sudden death after 23 years, and having been so lucky, I thought it wasn't likely I'd marry again, since I wasn't willing to settle for less.

Neither Matt nor I was looking for a primary relationship but just seemed to flow into one, on into living together for two years and then into marriage. Then retirement, and a move to California, where he had been visiting twice a year since 1969, and me with him after we met, so that we already had an established loving circle here and back East.

JUSTIN AND JASON (from Justin's point of view)

Here is another homosexual relationship, much more unusual than the previous one, because the lovers live 3,000 miles apart! Still, their love and joy are evident in this writing, and whenever I'm in their presence.

Our lifestyle may best be described as fast-paced, hectic, stressful, exciting and fun. Now that you have a lot of worthless adjectives, let me be more specific: I (you can call me Justin; might as well make up a name I like) am a securities lawyer with a large national law firm which represents some of the largest financial institutions in the United States. I have been practicing for four years and am at the point where I basically run very large deals on my own. Jason (he always wanted to be called Jason) is a strategic planner for a very large, well-known financial company. I live and work in Orange County, in Southern California. Jason lives and works in New York City. We both work for very demanding clients, in sophisticated financial transactions which require both a great deal of substantive knowledge and an ability to deal with people, both "bosses" and subordinates. We both spend a lot of time running from meeting to meeting and phone call to phone call, both work sixty-plus hours per week and are both highly paid (for our age).

One of us travels to the other's side of the continent at least once a month, usually for a three-day weekend. When I go to New York, I often arrive at two or three in the morning. When Jason returns home after a visit, he usually gets into

The City at six in the morning, goes home for a shower and shave and goes to the office for a full day. The weekends going back and forth are exhausting.

Our lovestyle is intense but quiet. Because we spend relatively little time together, there is not a lot of room for other people when we are together. We go to dinner alone, sit quietly at Jason's apartment with a movie, talk and make love. Often, it takes a little time to get to know each other again, and it can be mildly awkward when we first get together. There have been rare occasions when we are on such different wavelengths that we miss each other the whole time we are together. We are both learning to understand this, however, and talk about it openly. Because we are able to communicate freely (usually), problems don't become major disasters.

Jason also likes to entertain, however, and has a lot of friends (now *our* friends) who vie for our time, so we usually agree in advance how much time we'll allow other people, and generally stick to it. Having other people around lets us be a "couple," though, and that's nice and also helpful for our development as social animals, as well as useful in putting necessary space between us.

Communication plays a major role in our relationship. We talk on the telephone nearly every day—sometimes for a long time and others just for a few minutes. We have learned to tell each other when we're distracted by other things, usually work, so that we both understand that a "weird" phone conversation had nothing to do with the other person, and we don't panic. We can tell each other we're busy and are able to hang up without bothering the other, or feeling shut out. We're also very free, however, to call each other for moral support, or to whine, or to discuss ideas or ask advice, and also just to "cuddle" over the phone. It's often amazing how much besides just sound can be transmitted through telephone wires.

Our lifestyle and lovestyle mesh well because the former is fast-paced and frenetic and the latter lets us slow down and relax, although it requires us to run around a lot (i.e., to airports) in order to relax. If we were living together, or even close, I think there would be a tendency to demand more of each other's time, which there is already too little of, and additional stress would be put on the relationship.

To me, our current lifestyle is pretty satisfying, about a 7 or 8, the distance and the time apart being all that keep it from being a 10. The most satisfying aspect of our lifestyle is twofold: (1) We both have the opportunity to grow independently and develop our careers and our lives; and (2) we have the opportunity to work out some difficult problems because of the distance and the time apart, and thus the relationship grows stronger all the time. At the point we are able to live together, the hassles of day-to-day living should be relatively easy to deal with (although there is a whole new set of hassles with living together, I'm sure).

The thing I would most like to change is the amount of time we spend together. While our present way of doing things is exciting, it would be nice to curl up with Jason more often than three nights a month, and to see his face every day. At present we are simply pursuing our respective careers and letting things work out as they are supposed to. We find that if we push it, it only tends to be frustrating.

In this relationship, it was not very difficult to figure out what would work for us. Basically we determined at the out-set that we would have to play it by ear and count on things working out in the way we both wanted. Things have basically worked quite well.

Our present love/lifestyle would probably not have worked for me before now. I have learned a lot, particularly since an earlier (my first) relationship ended, about my own needs for attention, companionship and self-fulfillment. Without this knowledge, I would not have been able to deal with the distance and the time apart.

MARGO AND HAL (from Margo's point of view)

This is one of those relationships that looks very traditional from the outside. They've been through a lot together and have emerged smiling.

My husband Hal and I have had a successful, rewarding, deeply intimate and sexually open marriage for the past eight years. This statement seems, to most people who hear it, full of contradictions—but those who know us well, and we who are best able to judge, can attest to its validity.

After twenty-five years of a good, conventional marriage, Hal chose to go on his own; it was, in fact, on the eve of our twenty-sixth anniversary that he moved around our house, picking out lamps and spatulas for his own apart-ment. We were apart for almost a year, and then reunited.

A few months later, I admitted to Hal that I wanted to have an open relationship. "My God! I'd never have dared to suggest it!" he exclaimed.

I didn't want to return to the closed glass jar that our marriage had become, where our friends, all of the same age, religion, and social status, hid their real feelings and frustrations, their problems and passions, behind the "couple" facade.

Although I wanted very much to be Hal's wife forever, I missed the excitement, the adventure, the spontaneity of the wider world I had discovered while we were apart. Could we somehow have it all?

It wasn't easy to establish a way of life that included friends of the opposite sex for both of us. Eventually, we became part of a loosely organized group of "new age" people who valued self-awareness and variety, who sought to integrate their sexuality into the other aspects of their lives and personalities—a loving community of creative, supportive friends who shared their feelings deeply and honestly. They are both older and much younger than we are, wealthy and unemployed, poets, therapists, and taxi drivers, married couples and singles alone or in committed relationships, open or monogamous.

Among them we have formed several deep connections. I've been in a relationship for four years with Peter, a uniquely intelligent, spiritual, sensual man who has given me new insights into my self, my marriage and the world. He and Hal are good friends, and Peter is a welcome guest in our home.

Hal has had a series of relationships, some lasting as long as two years. If his friend was married, her husband has known about Hal; our openness precludes "cheating," either on each other or on anyone else.

Have there been problems? Indeed, during several crises it seemed that our marriage might end. Sometimes, Hal blithely assumed that "everything was acceptable" because

we had only good intentions toward each other. Other issues arose (or were they the same ones?) from my need to
feel "in control"—times when I wanted to veto Hal's choice
of a friend, to limit the hours he spent with her or the
length of a trip they took together. I feared that I was being "taken advantage of" by Hal, that something disastrous
would happen if he had his way; yet *he* always left *me* free
to make my own decisions. Somehow, we worked through
these issues and found a viable way of life.

What does it require to follow such an out-of-the-ordinary
path? Essentially, each partner must have a sturdy sense of
self-esteem, a sure knowledge of his/her own worth alone
and in the relationship. Both partners must be committed
to staying together and working through any problems. And
a sense of humor helps—the logistics often become ridicu-
lously complicated, or we realize that the true "infidelity"
is going to see the best movie in town with someone else.

How do we overcome jealousy and possessiveness? We can
only answer that we love each other so deeply that we each
want the other to know the pleasure of a close bond with
another person. We appreciate each other (I'd love to have
romantic, tender, supportive Hal for a lover if we weren't
married!) and we share an intensely passionate one-ness,
with far more honest communication than most couples
ever know. We can't imagine closing down our life again,
when we share so much satisfaction "the way we are."

SCOTT AND LEWIS (from Scott's point of view)

*Through all his growth and development, Scott has been a
student and a friend. The only thing he cannot convey here
is his highly original creativity and sense of humor. This*

259

young man went from being afraid to assert himself to hang-gliding and entrepreneuring—two great leaps of faith in himself. What fun to watch him go!

Describing my lifestyle is turning out to be much harder than I thought. I've started this several times, and it always seems to not tell the whole story. I suspect that the final version will not tell everything there is to tell about my lifestyle.

I am a gay man, a self-employed photographer, a man living with another gay man who is a very close friend and my lover. I am also a vegetarian, a gymnastic student and a person searching for spiritual enlightenment. I read a lot of different material, ranging from the I *Ching* to Shirley MacLaine to Tina's first book. All have helped me along the path I am choosing.

I am a self-employed photographer, having started my business a little over a year ago (with Tina's assistance, encouragement and her strong sense of business ethics). It is going well and everyday I realize how much I like doing photography and how I like setting my own hours, my own wages (there have been times of feast and famine) and my own rules of business. In short, I like having my own business. I am in a relationship that is working very well right at the moment. I started that relationship shortly after I started my business (last year certainly was a good one for me!). Again, I feel as if I am in control within that relationship. I'm choosing what I want out of it, and with the continued communication between myself and Lewis (my lover), I am sure that things can only get better.

The thing I like most about my lifestyle is that I am choosing it. It is a fluidic lifestyle. When something about it doesn't work, I change that part. I'm really starting to learn how to have my life go in a direction that I am choosing and I am so excited by that. I spend a lot of time thinking about what it is that I want, both in my lovestyle and lifestyle. (You can't have what you want if you don't KNOW what you want!) I have learned over the past two years (and hope I am continuing to learn) many effective ways to obtain those things that I want in my life. The simplest of these ways is just to ask. It took me a long time to learn what may seem so obvious, but if I ask for help with my business, someone usually will help. If I ask my lover for a back rub, I usually get it. I spent much time in the past not getting what I wanted because I expected people to read my mind. The best of friends, even the best of lovers, are usually not mind-readers, but even casual friends are very often willing to do something to help or to make your life better if you just ask in a non-demanding way.

My lovestyle and lifestyle go together very well. For one thing they are completely independent (well, almost) from each other. When one is not going as well as I would like, it has very little effect on the other. My love problems don't interfere with my work, and my work doesn't infringe on my love life. That feels real good because so far both have not had problems at the same time. If my business gets slow and I panic over money, I have a good love life and a supportive lover to get me through that time. If I have an argument with Lewis, I put my energy into my work until I am calm enough to discuss things rationally. The other thing, as I said before, is that they are going in a direction I am choosing. If something goes right, I give myself credit for having accomplished it. If something is less than the way I want it to be, I know I am the only one who can change it and make it right. That is a wonderful feeling to be in control of my own life.

There were times when what I have now was just a dream. It seemed so far away and so unattainable. Now that I have most of what I want, it seems so easily accomplished, at least in retrospect. I believe that what I have accomplished has not been difficult. It just took practice. I practiced having lovers until I got it right. I practiced working until I knew enough to work on my own. I am still practicing having my own business. Practice makes perfect.

The thing that I don't have now and that seems to be the next thing to work on is having other intimate relationships in addition to the lover I have now. I'm not sure yet whether what I want is occasional sexual encounters outside of my relationship, or perhaps something ongoing with someone else, maybe even between the three of us. Not knowing is, I am sure, a major reason why I have not yet accomplished that. Once I know what it is that I am looking for, I think it will work out. These are not the easiest times to play around sexually. They are not the easiest of times to have relationships of an alternative style. But once I know what I want, I know I will just need to practice, and sooner or later (probably sooner) it will be a part of my lifestyle and lovestyle.

BOB AND SARA JANE

Here are a couple who have been successfully through major transitions: from monogamous to open relationship, from parents to having grown children move away from home. They work together well, and they are a pleasure to know. I find their story eloquently put:

SARA JANE

Having been married twenty-seven years, I can see that my lifestyle, and to some degree lovestyle, directly correlates to my growth as an individual. When we had been married for twelve years, we decided to experiment with open marriages. Having been very traditional, this created a variety of feelings: loss of control, hurt, anger, jealousy. It also allowed me to become more aware of myself in relationship to other men. I learned more about myself sexually, emotionally and about my need to grow as an individual. My style was to put most of my energy into my relationship with my husband and occasionally spend time with one other man. The friendship was the most important part to me. My husband and I were both growing and changing, and it was very difficult at times.

At this point in my life I have come to the conclusion:

Loving people is something I choose to do.

Adding sex to that love tends to jerk me around emotionally unless I control the degree of intimacy.

I have decided not to be sexually involved with other men.

However, I have an eleven-year relationship with a man and it still involves sex, because it always has.

My relationship with my husband has gradually improved over the years. We have worked at resolving our differences in lovestyles. The other relationship meets some of my individual style, and I put less pressure on my husband.

263

Each of us being aware that we create our own reality (feelings, etc.) and are not victims has been a big help. We each look at our own part in the problem.

We spend significant time together and feel good about us.

My husband has another relationship (three years), but his obsession with his computer bothers me more. I find it easier to deal with the other relationship.

I am told ahead of time when he will see her. She goes to events with us if she chooses, and my friend has been included, too. However, over the years, in order for his wife to deal with our relationship, I have been totally excluded from his family. In the beginning she agreed to this type of lifestyle. Although it's difficult, the friendship seems unrealistic to give up.

At times I have been frustrated and angry, but set my own limits and gradually accept and enjoy whatever form it takes.

BOB

I have worked through feelings of abandonment and jealousy to get on the other side. I have gained an appreciation of the resiliancy of the human spirit to bounce back from great pain to love and appreciation and of the depth of emotion that is possible!

I get a clearer picture of my personality style by having more than one intimate relationship. The result is a perspective that my issue is my issue and not your problem.

A major life issue for me is projecting my judgment of myself onto others. I am learning to love more completely—unconditional love.

I have dispelled the myth of a perfect princess who would rescue me and discovered there is no personal growth in comparing and judging others, or expecting others (women) to provide fulfillment.

I have learned that:

> Satisfaction is not in form.
> There are variations of intimate love.
> Love is a complex and varied process—the style relates to the situation.
> For me it is a growth challenge to be intimate with a woman who is not my "partner."

HELEN, STAN AND JANET

Stan comes by his expertise as I do, by using his own life as his research laboratory. These are such loving people! Through their workshops, they heal much of the pain of their fellow human beings. I am proud to know them.

STAN

Attempting to describe the lifestyle that the three of us live is very much like asking a fish if it is swimming in water, or humans if they are aware that they are breathing air every second they are alive.

The answer for the three of us is, we are! We simply are living in love. So therefore our lovestyle touches everything we do, everything we think and say.

Let me explain. Helen and I have been married twenty-nine years. Janet and I have been married nine years. (Because you can't legally have two spouses in our free society, Helen is "legal," Janet is "extra-legal.") Helen, Janet and I got married to each other "extra-legally" three years ago in Jamaica, and six months ago the three of us got a new house and started living together.

Because we are in love together, everything we do and say comes from a place of love. Some of the basic ingredients of our love are: dignity, respect, understanding of needs, wants and desires, and most importantly—trust. Trust is our "Rock of Gibraltar." It is the very foundation of our relationship. We trust each other! We love each other! We truly don't believe people can really love each other without trust. To us they are totally synonymous. Love is trust. Trust is love. Also synonymous is unconditional. Unconditional is love. Love is unconditional. The minute one condition is placed on the other person, it is the equivilent of saying, I will love you *if*.

There can be no IF's in a loving relationship, because the way we see it, I = Ignorance, F = Fear. Ignorance and fear are the greatest enemies of humanity. So everytime we even think of "if," we translate it immediately to, What aren't we aware of, and what are we afraid of? What we have been able to observe is that fear is strictly a negative fantasy/thought. If that happens, then we immediately check out what the negative fantasy/thought is all about. If there is no validity to it, and there hasn't been so far, we immediately throw it—the thought—into the garbage can where it really belongs.

So, as we see it, our lifestyle and our lovestyle totally mesh. Every little thing is an expression of our lifestyle. We are indeed living a loving lifestyle. Furthermore, because we have a bigger, more all-encompassing purpose for our lives—the enrichment and transformation of the planet—we never run out of purpose, which is the dynamo providing the extra added energy that propels our relationship forward.

Giving each other "things" is a very nice gesture, but it is never equated with love, any more than any other thing in our lives. It has been our observation that many people give each other things because they want something in return, and that gift really then comes from an insecure place. We want their attention, and approbation is the motivator for the gift. However, when you are living love, every word, look, thought and action is a total expression of love.

Nothing in anything that has been said above is to equate love with like. I can love you, and not like what you do. The best example of the above statement is the parent/child relationship. Many times parents don't like what their children do, but it is the rare parent who withdraws their love because they don't like what their child does. Even if the child becomes a criminal, murderer, dope addict or rapist, most parents still don't withdraw their love from their children. However, the same cannot, unfortunately, be said about most married people, or those living in varied lifestyles. If there is something that one of us does that we don't like, the first thing we do (or as soon as possible) is confront the person about their behavior. We use the "no-response technique." That is, the person responding must be listened to, without any interruptions, except for clarification. When they have completed, the same courtesy is extended to all others in the conversation. That way, everyone is assured of being heard. I can honestly say that there aren't too many things any of us have done that the others haven't liked, and when those times have occurred, they have been handled gently and with compassion.

To say that we find our loving lifestyle satisfying is equivalent to saying that the wonders of the world are just O.K. We, I, all of us think that it is the best thing ever, and ranks alongside the wonders of the world. What baffles us is why more people aren't living it? Everything about it is appealing, as well as life- and love-affirming. We think we are three of the luckiest people on this or any other planet. I wouldn't change a single, solitary thing about it, except would have started it much earlier. Of course, I realize that wasn't possible, because each minute of our lives to this point was a rehearsal for this fantastic event.

I can honestly say that there never was a time that I didn't realize that I/we were on the right path. So, for me, there wasn't the slightest bit of a struggle. On the other hand, Helen experienced some problems of a personal nature: self-identity, self-image concerns. Having had a role model or two probably would have made things a bit easier, but I'm sure not as much fun.

I think all relationships continuously evolve. Not always in a positive direction, but evolve they do. Sometimes the shift is miniscule, other times very dramatic. Even so-called standard relationships keep changing, but it seems that most are outer-directed as opposed to the inner-direction that most aware lifestyles follow. So, for me, starting out as an arch-conservative war hawk, etc., my lifestyle never would have been thinkable back then, let alone work. The changes have varied from the subtle to the profound over the years. My first wife was a Born-Again Christian who made Billy Graham seem like an atheist. Helen pretty much resembled me in choice of lifestyle and beliefs twenty-nine years ago. My relationship with Helen has undergone terrific transformation over the years. Janet was born for a loving lifestyle. She is truly the woman of the now and the future. She just lives, breathes, eats and drinks love.

In conclusion, although our lifestyle might not be for everyone, wouldn't it be wonderful in this advanced age of ours, if each person could choose the lifestyle that they felt best suited them without tons of disapproval both from government and individuals? With love as scarce as it appears for the general population, it would seem that we should encourage love and loving, no matter what the form, as long as the content was pure love.

JANET

To describe my lifestyle on one hand is so easy: I have 100% love and a 100% love of life. On the other hand, it isn't always easy to describe, being as I have chosen to love more than one person. That I do it is easy for me; to explain it so reactions don't scare or chase people away is another thing.

I was raised to think I would fall in love, get married and live happily ever after, not being told about the inbetween stuff—responsibilities, money, raising kids, how to be potent and honest. Maybe being a girl made a difference. I wasn't told to overtly lie, but there were ways a female *should* act and be. Don't make important decisions, be almost mindless and just agree.

From the beginning I knew that was not for me. So I set out to learn all that I could. Especially about people, relationships and myself. I have loved my evolving into a woman. I have found I can love a man, Stan, who is currently married to Helen, whom I also love, support and am in heart married to also. I am also in heart married to Stan. I don't have a piece of paper given by the state saying we are legally married. That piece of paper wouldn't change our love and what it stands for. Our nine years together have been the most beautiful and fulfilling times I've ever known.

It isn't always easy or comfortable for people to hear that I cherish this 300% relationship and wouldn't want to be doing anything else. It requires everything that a one-on-one relationship takes. Maybe a little more so. The best part is knowing and feeling the love given me and not needing it proven, and having my love received and not having to prove it. Yet I love showing my love in many ways.

If communication isn't clear, a good look at our course direction is viewed and cleared up. But this seems to be a rare event because we are always looking at our journey and making sure our course is in the direction we all want.

It hasn't been a struggle for me in our lovestyle because I am clear with myself and the people in my life. I am not dependent—don't need to be taken care of. Yet I am open to being a loving, caring, sharing, open-to-life person. I want people in my life, especially ones with the same ingredients. That is what I have created for myself, as well as for the people I have in my life.

I find we are changing and growing together. We learn a lot from each other. Especially, how to love unconditionally. I would never hurt Helen or Stan or anyone in my life. If our relationship hurt Helen, I wouldn't be in it. There is always understanding, consideration and compassion.

I am proud of my lifestyle/lovestyle. It works for all of us fantastically. So many facets of our relationship could apply to any type of relationship. *Neither one right, neither one wrong!* It's just heart-based, with pure love. And in fact I did *fall in love, get married, and am living happily ever after!*

RICHARD AND TINA (from Tina's point of view)

After having described many details of the lovestyle Richard and I live, I thought it only fair to describe our lifestyle, too.

Richard and I have been married for five years, after dating for four months, and living together for four months more. Richard is a bisexual man and has been all his life. We met at a party given by the Bisexual Center of Southern California (also known as Arete). The party we met at was a "permissive" weekend party, meaning sex was OK at the party as long as the guidelines were followed. So I knew he was bisexual from the start, and we both got involved in a threesome with another man that weekend. The three of us had an ongoing dating arrangement for three months, during which time Richard and I became more and more deeply involved as a couple. Eventually, the other man got involved elsewhere, and though we're all still friends, we're no longer intimate.

Our marriage is sexually open, and Richard "dates" far more often than I do. We are actively looking for a third partner for our marriage who could/would eventually be equal in the relationship. We sometimes refer to ourselves as a "single couple," which is only partly a joke. We fairly often have threesomes with another man, and we've had a couple of foursomes with other couples. Although I have had sexual contact with women on a couple of occasions, I do not at this time feel that I am bisexual. My gay friends say I'm "biemotional," or "bent," as opposed to "straight" or "gay."

Richard and I have sex on an average of about six or seven times a week, which is plenty for me, so when he dates, or goes out looking, I usually spend time with my very close friends. I have many long-time friendships, in which I am heavily involved, and get much pleasure from them. Sometimes I just welcome the time to be alone and write or relax.

It's OK in our arrangement for me to date, too, although I've had only three dates in our four years together, because it's not a high priority. There are times when I perceive Richard as "uptight" and I suggest he go out, because that always seems to relax him and enhance our time together.

Both of us have a very open lovestyle in which we enjoy a variety of people and activities, and we like lots of new adventures in our lives. We're high-energy people anyway, each of us owning our own business and with very active schedules. We've both studied spiritually and metaphysically, and unconditional love has a high value for us. We feel that the more people involved, the greater the possibilities for love. There's also a powerful metaphysical interpretation to the number three that we would like to explore in relationship to love.

This style is very experimental, and that suits us, because we like the excitement and the challenge. Also, we have the luxury of businesses that are not adversely affected by the controversy of our lifestyle. There's no temptation to remain "closeted," and sharing, teaching and personal growth are all high values and priorities for us. Anyone who has read *How to Be a Couple and Still Be Free* knows that freedom and cooperation are high personal values for me.

This lifestyle suits my personal lovestyle perfectly. The only change I'm motivated to seek is to be open to the natural changes that are necessary as we learn and grow. It would also be fun to find "Prince Charming II" and experience the change he would bring. Change excites rather than worries me, and I remain as consciously open as I can to the possibilities.

My whole life so far has been a journey to where I am, and only in the last ten years have I learned to live and grow emotionally without major struggle. I have had to experiment and learn on my own, because the social rules I knew felt crazy and toxic to me. What did make it easier was my teachers, all wise and wonderful people, beginning with my father, who said, "I don't care what you think [although I think he might be shocked now], as long as you think for yourself." Also, all of my loves have been incredibly helpful in pointing out my pathway, even when they appeared to be "the problem."

I think more information about real life, such as the Marriage and Family classes in high schools today, would have been very helpful, saving me time in discovering that love and marriage were not "happily ever after," and that success in relationships requires skill and knowledge.

I would not have been ready for Richard or a truly open and honest relationship much before I met him. He says the same about me. We are both powerful personalities, and we each require someone equally strong and grounded. It took nearly forty years for me to achieve the necessary growth. I spent a long time feeling that whatever was going on was OK, as long as I didn't have to hear about it.

My changes in lifestyle/lovestyle have coincided with my partners', and it's probably a "which-came-first" question. I did experience several different style experiments with the relationship I had from 1972–78. He and I seemed to have gotten together expressly for the purpose of experimentation. We were never really settled into one lifestyle for an unbroken time. He was one of my greatest teachers.

Just as I've changed careers and felt enhanced by the change, each new relationship has enhanced my life. I'm hoping now, with my knowledge and capacity for smooth transition, that Richard and I will share many changes; however, since I come from a long-lived line, I do expect to outlive him, and that will be another transition. With the exception of inevitable death, I would like to *add* new people from now on, rather than *change to* new people.

I hope this sampler of experiences has been sufficient to impress you with the variety and richness possible in relationships, and with the fact that people need different styles and will create individual solutions, *whether they feel "weird" about it or not.*

Shoulds, rules, restrictions and criticism cannot prevent you from being as creative as you need to be; they just make it harder for you to recognize your appropriate solutions.

One last time I'd like to say that I don't believe there is a single lifestyle that's right for everyone. It's imperative to your emotional security that you accept this and make the necessary adjustments to what you think you "should" do, so that you can find out what will really work for you.

I leave you with Timothy Leary's advice (although I don't agree with all his philosophy, I *love* this one): *"Think for yourself—question authority."*

I wish you love and joy, in whatever forms you like.

READING RESOURCES

Relationships

Friedman, Sonya. *Men Are Just Desserts*. Warner Books, 1983.
Goldberg, Herb. *The Hazards of Being Male*. Signet, 1980.
———. *The New Male-Female Relationship*. Signet, 1983.
Keyes, Ken. *A Conscious Person's Guide to Relationships*. Loveline, 1975.
Tessina, Tina B. & Riley K. Smith. *How to Be a Couple and Still Be Free*. Newcastle, 1980.

Personal Development and Consciousness

Dale, Stan & Val Beauchamp, *Fantasies Can Set You Free*. Celestial Arts, 1980.
Gawain, Shakti. *Creative Visualization*. Whatever Publishing, 1978.
——— with Laurel King. *Living in the Light*. Whatever Publishing, 1986.
Golas, Thaddeus. *The Lazy Man's Guide to Enlightenment*. Bantam, 1980.
Hay, Louise. *You Can Heal Your Life*. Hay House, 1984.
Keyes, Ken. *Prescriptions for Happiness*. Loveline, 1975.
MacLaine, Shirley. *Dancing in the Light*. Bantam, 1985.
———. *Out on a Limb*. Bantam, 1984.
Ray, Sondra. *I Deserve Love*. Celestial Arts, 1976.

Fiction About Alternate Lifestyles

Alexander, Thea. *2150 A.D.* Warner Books, 1971.
Bradley, Marion Zimmer. *Thendara House*. DAW Books, 1985.
Bryant, Dorothy. *The Kin of Ata Are Waiting for You*. Moon Books, 1976.
LeGuin, Ursula K. *The Dispossessed*. Avon, 1974.